LIBRARY MANAGEMENT

RECENT THOUGHTS AND DEVELOPMENT

LIBRARY MANAGEMENT

RECENT THOUGHTS AND DEVELOPMENT

DR. SUBODH GOPAL NANDI
University Librarian
Visva-Bharati, Santiniketan, West Bengal

2011
Kaveri Books
New Delhi - 110 002

First Published in 2011

ISBN : 978-81-7479-115-3

Published by

Kaveri Books

4832/24, Ansari Road, Darya Ganj
New Delhi-110002 (India)

Tel : 011-23288140, 23245799
Telefax : 011-2382 8140
E-mail : kaveribooks@vsnl.com
web : www.kaveribooks.com

Printed at
Salasar Imaging Systems, Delhi - 110 052

PRINTED IN INDIA

Dedication

To

My Three Daughters
Sumana, Sudarshana & Suranjana

Acknowledgement

I am very happy to announce that the publication "Library Management : Recent Thoughts and Development" has come out successfully. I am really thankful to Mr. Rakesh Goel of Kaveri Books, New Delhi for publishing this work within a very short time. I would like to convey my thanks to the editors of different journals on Library and Information Science and editors of different Seminar/Conference Proceedings in which some topics of the present work have been selected and published.

I should acknowledge my family members for maintaining their assistance to complete this work. Special thanks are due to Sumana, my elder daughter who is engaged for the Ph.D. work in Astrophysics as DST fellow at ARIES, Nainital and now staying at NCRA, Pune for Radio Astronomical observation and analysis of date, etc. I receive her continuous encouragement for completion of this work. I am thankful to Visva-Bharati Library and all staff members for helping me during my work.

Dr. Subodh Gopal Nandi
Central Library, Visva-Bharati

Preface

The library, from its beginning is known as a social instrument. The library presupposes the existence of literature, which was preserved in ancient times on clay tablets. Afterwards, papyrus, parchment or paper has been used as medium of recording of human knowledge. So the earliest forms of libraries do not fit with our modern ideas and notions of the library, because the shape, in which human records of knowledge have been recorded, stored or arranged and used were different from place to place and from time to time.

Modern ideas of libraries and library services have deep roots in Middle Ages. The structures and services that can be found in 20th century libraries began to take shape in the early 17th century. Modern libraries are the storehouse of recorded human knowledge, which are of different types *i.e.* books, manuscripts, maps, reports, patents, microfiches, microfilms, etc. These physical objects of recorded human knowledge are of different subjects, different times, different ages, different lingual, different countries, and that have different medium of recording but arranged scientifically. It is true that men are using different items in different times for their recording of knowledge. It is also true that men are using different medium for their knowledge recording. All these changes have a history, which is always be remembered by the librarians as the organization and management of libraries have always been influenced by these changes. The library that has several items of human knowledge is beyond the traditional library and should be handled in different way and in complex manner.

So it is a great challenge to librarians how efficiently he/she could manage his/her library where physical objects of the library collection are heterogeneous and library users are of varied interests. Recently libraries have entered in an age where flow of information or searching of information have no longer been definable in geographical area or terms; but rather have international phenomena based on increased use of Information Technology and its applications. Publishers are now using communication technologies for their information products.

Thus the new vision has been created in the field of library and information centre, which influences for taking some positive steps for modification library management system. As a university librarian I have noticed that some changed topics are basically coming to the library due to present day influence of technological development and the society. I am facing this challenge of changing scenario and taking some measures to cope up or to tackle the present changing library situation. This recent changing environment of library has influenced me to undertake some experimentation which representing as the final output of the present work "Library Management : Recent Thoughts and Development."

The present work contains 13 chapters which are all related to current topics on library management and services. These chapters include discussions on trends in library management; job satisfaction of library professionals; library and its working group; library profession and code of ethics; library and information services in e-library environment; open source software and its application; e-publications as helpful resources for researchers; developing skills of library professionals for using ICT; application of knowledge management; copy right; electronic recording technology; managing university libraries in changing environment; and knowledge preservation on Indigenous System of Medicine. Almost all chapters have two elements of specified discussion : the theoretical implication and their application rudiments.

The present work is basically talks about recent thoughts and development of libraries; and I am sure that the present work would immense helpful for the librarians and all those who are associated with the Library and Information Science Education as teachers, researchers and students.

Santiniketan
Central Library

Dr. Subodh Gopal Nandi
University Librarian, Visva-Bharati

Contents

Acknowledgment (*vi*)

Preface (*vii*)

1. Current Trends in Library Management 1
2. Job Satisfaction of the Library Professionals 7
3. Library and its Working Group : a Study 16
4. Library Profession and its Code of Ethics 26
5. Changing Dimensions of Library and Information Services in E-Library Environment 34
6. Open Source Softwares and Their Applications in Libraries 45
7. E-Publications as Helpful Resources for Researchers of Indian Libraries 53
8. Developing Skills of Library Professionals for Using Information and Communication Technology (ICT) 65
9. Application of Knowledge Management in Library and Information Centre 75
10. Copy Right, Library and Library Services 87
11. Library and Electronic Recording Technology (ERT) 96
12. Managing University Library in Changing Environment 106
13. Knowledge Preservation on Indigenous System of Medicine 121

Index 135

Chapter 1

Current Trends in Library Management

Library is a service oriented complex organization. Those persons who are involved in this organization as employee have some good academic background or otherwise, they have at least minimum educational background. So, here, in this organization, management style is different to any other industrial organization. The main objective of this chapter is to establish a standard management style which the library manager can adopt for the successful accomplishment of the existing and future goal and objective of his/her library.

1. Library and its Manager

Library is an organization, which builds up with certain exceptions, provides certain need fulfillment opportunities, and controls certain actual and potential behaviours. As the library organizations are built on functional unit, its managers (Librarian = Library Manager) are centrally involved in managing the interface between the work of the library organization and the skills of the employee. The library managers also manage the motivation of their employees to gain the objective of the library organization in its highest degree. So, the library managers must create a relationship between employees and the library so that their subordinates are willing to expend energy on the organizational task.

2. Library and its Employee

Here we may say, library is a system and individual is also another system, and the library manager plays a great role, and who conjoins the two systems. The organization, library, has certain goal, purpose and objective. And again, an individual has it's own particular needs. These two different systems enter into a joint and co-operation ship only when it offers opportunities for the fulfillment of their needs. Otherwise, it may be said, the organization (the Library) employs the individual because his services are essential for the achievement of its goals, purposes and objectives; and similarly, the individual (employee) contributes his services only when it leads or directs to the fulfillment of his personal needs. So there exists a reciprocal relationship.

3. Reciprocal Relationship

This reciprocal relationship between the organization (library) and its employee is based on psychological contract. It is called psychological because much of it is unwritten and unverbalised. When the library and its employee enters into this reciprocal relationship, both parties bring to the relationship a set of expectations what each will give and receive.

3.1 Examples of Expectations

The following are the illustrative areas in which the organization[1] and the individual are likely to have expectations:

What the individual may expect to receive and the organization may expect to give :	*What the individual may expect to give and the organization may expect to receive :*
(*a*) Salary;	(*a*) An honest days work;
(*b*) Personal development;	(*b*) Loyalty to organization;
(*c*) Recognition and approval for good work; Security through fringe benefits;	(*c*) Initiative;
(*d*) Friendly, supportive environment;	(*d*) Conformity to organizational norms;
(*e*) Fair treatment; and	(*e*) Job effectiveness; and
(*f*) Meaningful or purposeful job.	(*f*) Flexibility and willingness to learn and to develop.

Noragh Jones and Peter Jordan[2] have observed this employer-employee relationship in a different way. They argued that there may well be a conflict between the aims of the employers and the aims of the employees, and this is very obvious constrain in the business of trying to achieve a healthy balance between concern for output and concern for people:

Aims of the Employer	*Aims of the Employee*
Work specificity;	Work flexibility;
Output;	Input;
Uniformity; and	Individuality; and
Performance (What one does)	Personal qualities (What one is)

4. Role of Library Manager

Here, the library manager partakes a fruitful role and he is the person who is most responsible for implementing this psychological contract. The library manager provides an organizational design, which facilitates the performance of organizational tasks and goals; again, this organizational design ensures employees to realize their expectations at work[3]. The above is always true in every functional organization.

The role of Library manager, in this connection, can be shown diagrammatically thus :

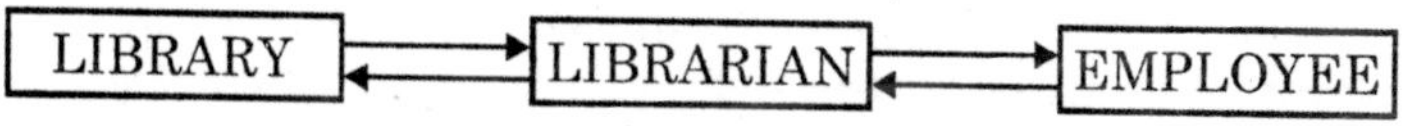

Fig. 1 : Reciprocal relationship between the organisation (Library) and its employees.

5. McGregor's Theory – X & Theory – Y

Among the several management theories the library manager may consider Douglas McGragor's 'X – Y' theory[4] in the field of library organization.

The theory X assumes that employees are on the whole indolent. They lack ambition and are resistant to change. They have an inherent dislike of work and will avoid it, if possible. Because of this human characteristics of dislike for work, and are self centered and indifferent to organizations need. These people have to be controlled, directed or threatened with punishment to get them to put forth adequate effort towards the achievement of organizational objectives or goals.

There can be both a 'hard' and a 'soft' approach by the management. The hard approach involves very tight inspection, checking and control and even threatened by the management in order to get them to put forth an adequate effort. There is little communication except downwards from seniors to juniors. Again, the soft approach involves in speaking softly but till using the 'carrot and stick' approach by the management. Employees normally take advantage of a soft approach and their performance get worse. They continually expect more, but they give less and less.

McGragor argues that the 'Carrot and Stick' approach is a means that satisfies the employee's physical and their safety (within limits) needs or the lower level needs. But this approach does not work at all once man has reached an adequate subsistence level and is motivated primarily by higher needs. This leads the people to frustration.

Against the 'theory – X', McGragor argued for 'theory – Y', which is actually an alternative theory, based on more adequate assumptions about human nature. External control and the threat of punishment are not the only means of inducing effort towards organizational objectives. Theory Y approach assumes that people will exercise self-correction and self-control in working towards objectives to which they are committed. It is the responsibility of management to create such condition that the employee is encouraged and enabled to fulfill themselves and satisfy their higher level needs for esteem, recognition and achievement. By their work operation employees not only achieve their own goals better, yet will contribute more to the goals of organization.

6. Applications to Libraries

In a real life situation in any organization one rarely finds such clear-cut positions, and very often, different departments or sections are characterized by different approaches. In a library organization a cataloguing or acquisition department or section might be managed along theory – X lines, while in the same library a team of subject specialists might be operating along theory – Y lines[5]. Theory – X and theory – Y may not be seen as parallel lines which never meet, but rather as opposite ends of a continuum. The library may follow a management line towards the hierarchic end of the scale, devoted to downward communication. But for information service, the same library can use lateral communication between people in different chains of hierarchy whose work is complementary but who are separated by the organizations management structure. It can circumvent management barriers to permit people to reach the information they themselves identify as necessary for their work rather than what their superior consider they need – and without unproductive superior/subordinate conflict.

7. Conclusion

Management is working with and through people in an effort to accomplish organizational goals. To achieve these goals by effective management, the library manager may think about the adaptation of MaGragor's X – Y theory, which is beneficial both to the library organization and personally in terms of work satisfaction.

References

1. Thomas, R.: Managing the psychological contract. *In* Lawrence, PR., *et al.:* Organisational Behaviour and Administration; cases and readings. 3rd ed. Homewood: Illinois, 1976, P. 465 – 480.

   [**Note** : Author has remarked that this discussion of psychological contract is based primarily on: Harry Levinson, et al. Men, management and mental health. Cambridge, Massachusetts: Harvard University Press, 1966. P. 22 – 38 and David J Lawless: Effective management: social psychological approach. Jew Jersey: Prentice Hall, 1972, P. 144 – 164].

2. Jones, N and Jordan, P. : Staff management in library and information work. Hampshire, England: Gower, 1982. P. 43.
3. Thomas, R.: Managing the psychological contract. *In* Lawrence, PR., *et al.:* Organisational Behaviour and Administration; cases and readings. 3rd.ed. Homewood: Illinois, 1976, P. 70-71.
4. McGragor, DM.: The human side of enterprise. *In* Lawrence, PR., *et. al.* : Organisational Behaviour and Administration;

cases and readings. 3rd ed. Homewood: Illinois, 1976, P. 506 – 515.

5. Jones, N and Jordan, P.: Staff management in library and information work. Hampshire, England: Gower, 1982. P. 36.

Chapter 2

Job Satisfaction of the Library Professionals

Job satisfaction is really a great problem in any organisational settings. The analysis of job satisfaction within an organisation is very helpful to assess the soundness or health of that organisation. The main objective of this chapter is to study some of the eminent studies on job satisfaction in library and some of their problems and to explore some methods of increasing job satisfaction.

1. Term Concept

The word 'job' means a piece of work to be done. It refers to a very specific task. The expression 'job satisfaction' means the satisfaction derived from a piece of work in which the person is engaged. It is essentially related to human needs and their fulfilment through work. Actually, job satisfaction is generated by individual's perception of how well his job on the whole is satisfying to his various needs. An individual tries to fulfil his wide variety of needs through his work.

Job satisfaction refers to the feelings and emotional aspects of individual's experience towards his job as different from intellectual or rational aspects. The experience of satisfaction or dissatisfaction with individual's work is the consequence of the extent of his positive or negative job attitudes. Job satisfaction is not a permanent attitude nor it is a momentary attitude. It is only a relatively enduring state which undergoes a change with the needs of individual, the capacity of work situation which fulfils these needs, and the individual's own perception of the situation.

N. Jones and E.P. Jordan[1] have studied job satisfaction in the library field in the following way :

An individual's sense of job satisfaction (or lack of it) does not depend solely on his or her own motivation (since for example, the individual alienated in the formal organisation may find fulfilment in union activity or in the sociability of the informal group). Nor does it depend only on the management styles and structures operating in the library. It is devolved rather from the nature of the task to be arrived at, the qualifications and the skills and attitudes of the person responsible, the nature of the other people in the library, and the management climate (compounded from the values, styles and interests of those who do the managing). Environmental factors are also important, since the rate of change in organization puts stuff under stress and threatens existing job satisfaction.

2. Definition

From the above discussion it is clear that it is not easy task to define job satisfaction. To define job satisfaction, M L Blum and J C Naylor[2] have said :

Job satisfaction is the result of various attitudes of the person holds toward the job, toward related factors and toward life in general.

According to Brown, Berrien and Russell[3] :

Job satisfaction is a favourable feelings or psychological condition of a person toward his job situation.

According to Tiffin and McCormick[4] :

Job satisfaction is influenced both by the extent to which the work of person does, is intrinsically interesting to him, and by his attitude toward total work situation, including the company, his supervisor and his fellow workers.

3. Methods of Job Satisfaction Study

There are some commonly used methods for studying job satisfaction of the workers or employees, *viz* (*i*) interview; (*ii*) attitude scales and questionnaires; (*iii*) direct observation; and (*iv*) projective techniques.

4. Studies on Job Satisfaction in Library Field

A larger number of studies on job satisfaction were carried out among librarians in Britain and the United States which have shown that library professional are motivated by similar factors to others professionals.

4.1 : Sheffield Manpower Project Study

A job satisfaction study, the Sheffield Manpower Project (1970)[5] which examined a sample of public, academic and librarians, has reported thus :

Preference was expressed for greater responsibility of various kinds; more freedom of choice, less choice supervision, and greater opportunity to improve and act in a solo capacity. Work restructuring and job enlargement techniques should be considered in order to try and meet this desire. This applies at all levels, including the most juniors. It especially applies in situations where duties have been rigidly divided into professional and non-professional categories.

4.2 : Plate and Stone Study

In another study, American librarians Plate and Stone[6] used 'Herzberg's theory'[7] on job motivation to examine factors affecting job satisfaction among 162 American and 75 Canadian librarians from all types of libraries. The results of this study confirmed Herzberg's views that certain factors are positive 'motivators' in the work place, while others are merely 'hygiene factors'. These hygiene factors create dissatisfaction, if absent in the work place but they are not the positive motivation. In this study it is found that of all the factors named by librarians as contributing to job satisfaction, 99 percent were motivators and were related to job content. Of all the factors contributing to their dissatisfaction at work, 81 percent involved hygiene factors found in the work environment (context factors).

The motivational factors or motivators have been identified as under :

1. Achievement;
2. Recognition;

3. Work itself;
4. Responsibility;
5. Advancement; and
6. Professional or personal growth.

The hygiene factors have been indentified as 'under' :

1. Institution policy and administration;
2. Supervision;
3. Interpersonal relationships;
4. Working conditions;
5. Status;
6. Salary; and
7. Security.

4.3 : Vaughn and Dunn Study

W.J. Vaughn and J.D. Dunn (1974)[8] have studied job satisfaction among the library employees who are employed in six university libraries. For this study they used Job Description Index. This Job Description Index asks the employee to describe their job environment, in six university libraries, in relation to five job characteristics :

1. Work itself;
2. Supervisory climate;
3. Interpersonal climate;
4. Pay conditions ; and
5. Promotion opportunities.

4.4 : Wabha Study

Susanne P Wabha (1975)[9] has studied job satisfaction among the librarian and she employed Need Satisfaction Questionnaire method for this study. In this study Wahba's conclusion was that female librarians are treated differently than their male counterparts and consequently experience less job satisfaction.

4.5 : George P D'elia Study

This study[10] seeks to identify those factors which are most highly related to job satisfaction among librarians. This study includes 224 librarians both male and female of five groups of librarians representative of the type of library in which the librarians worked. These groups are :

(*a*) Public services librarians in academic libraries;

(*b*) Technical services librarians in academic libraries;

(*c*) Public service librarians in public libraries;

(*d*) School librarians; and

(*e*) Special librarians.

Three measuring instruments are used here :

(*a*) MIQ [Minnesota Importance Questionnaire]–to measure vocational needs of the librarian;

(*b*) MJDQ [Minnisota Job Description Questionnaire]– to measure a librarian's perceptions of the characteristics of his job environment; and

(*c*) MSQ [Minnisota Satisfaction Questionnaire]–to measure a librarian's satisfaction with each of these job characteristics.

In this study it is found the job satisfaction among the librarians is not related to their sex, the type of the library in which they worked, or their vocational needs, but it is related to the characteristics of their job environments. Of these the supervisory climate and the intrinsic characteristics of the job itself are the two most important determinants of job satisfaction. It is experienced in this study, that there is an integral relationship between a supervisory climate which is conductive to the exercise of individual initiative and professional judgement and the librarian's experience of measuring a job. Thus, it tends to indicate that a participatory administrative style or perhaps even a laissez-faire style, is conductive to job satisfaction among librarians.

4.6 : Jones and Jordan on the Issue

A survey on job satisfaction among recently qualified graduates in libraries, Jones and Jordan[11] has reported frustration and disappointment caused by the following factors :

(*a*) Lack of opportunity to exercise one's professional expertise;

(*b*) Lack of opportunity to exercise responsibility;

(*c*) Dull and repetitive routine work, rather than a chance to use skills acquired during one's professional education; and

(*d*) Insufficient contact with users (staff deployed in technical services, and non-professional staff had more contact with users than professional staff), to sense of achievement is missing.

5. Problems

The above studies of job satisfaction of librarians reveal that there are many investigators working from varied theoretical positions, using numerous methods, and with different samples. Many of the studies of job satisfaction of librarians fail to specify the population which their subjects represent. In addition, they used some varied measuring instrument and question whether they are measuring the same attitudes. Questionnaires are apparently accepted on face validity, and little is reported of the reliability of either the criterion or the measure of attitudes. However, this may be due to our inadequacy at the present time to comprehend the influence of a wide range of variables, many of which are confounded.

6. Methods of Increasing Job Satisfaction

Herzberg has reached a conclusion on the basis of the motivational and hygience factors that employees feel motivated if the job is interesting and challenging; if the possibilities of growth exists in it; if they are able to obtain a sense of achievement; if they have the responsibility and authority to use their discretion; and if they are able to advance in the profession and receive recognition for the tasks they have done.

Generally, three methods, *viz* (*i*) job enrichment; (*ii*) job enlargement; and (*iii*) job rotation are used for increasing job satisfaction.

6.1 : Job Enrichment

It means, according to Luthans and Knod[12] designing jobs that include a greater work content; require a higher level of knowledge and skill; give the worker more autonomy and responsibility for planning, directing and controlling his own performance; and provide opportunity for personal and meaningful work experience.

In library work an example of job enrichment is in teh grouping of cataloguers, each person takes responsibility for a particular group of subjects, in which they all catalogue and classify. Job enrichment may be achieved by subject specialization structures in academic libraries.

6.2 : Job Enlargement

It is suggested by Argyris[13] in enlarging a job, *i.e.*, performing a variety of tasks or operations of the same task. Actually, it means adding other tasks of the same level to an employee's job, mainly to prevent tidiness (boredom).

In library work, persons involved in cataloguing when assigning special duty to organize periodical indexing services or counter duties, in absense of counter staff, etc. are the examples of job enlargement.

6.3 : Job Rotation

In this case the individual can be asked to perform only similar jobs. An individual may be engaged to work for a particular period on a particular job 'X', again for the same period another particular job 'Y', again on another job 'Z' etc., and then again he may be asked to come back to the first job 'X'.

In library routine works this method can be used on weekly, monthly or even annual basis.

7. Conclusion

In conclusion it may be said that characteristics of both the individual and the job appear to be related to job satisfaction, but they are intercorrelated to such an extent that it is extremely difficult to isolate them for scientific investigation. It is a good policy for any organisation to ensure job satisfaction which is able to generate a favourable climate of employee-employer strained relationship. Finally, it may be argued that job satisfaction is of the main cause which leads to a more effective functioning of the individuals and the organisation as a whole.

Library organisations and industrial organisation are not the same; industries are production oriented organisation but the libraries are service oriented organisations. Plate and Stone[14] in their survey of job satisfaction among American librarians has rightly remarked:

Libraries, despite their apparent homogeneity, differ considerably with regard to their organisational history, leadership climate, and even goals and objectives. Library procedures may vary from library to library and so must personnel practices and supervisory styles.... Library managers must therefore be skilled in the adaptation of existing principles of motivation to local requirements.

References

1. Jones, N. and Jordan, P. : Staff management is library and information work. Hamps Hire : Gower, 1982. p. 20-21.
2. Blum, M.L. and Naylor, J.C. : Industrial psychology : its theoretical and social foundations. New York : Hamper and Row, 1968. p. 353.
3. Brown, J.M., Berrien F.K. and Russell, D.L. : Applied psychology, New York : Macmillan 1966. p. 395.
4. Tiffin, Joseph and McCormick, Ernest J. : Industrial psychology. Ed 4. Calcutta : Asia, Publishing House, 1960, p. 317.
5. Sergean, R., McKay, J.R. and Corkill, C.M. : Sheffield Manpower Project: a survey of staffing requirements for librarianship and information work : Final Report. Shiffield: University of Sheffield Postgraduate School of Librarianship and Information Science, 1976. p. 293.

6. Plate, K.H. and Stone, E.W. : Factors affecting librarians' job satisfaction : a report of two studies. *Library Quarterly.* 44 (2) April 1974. p. 91-110.
7. Herzberg, F. : Work and the nature of man. New York : World Publishing, 1966.
8. Vaughn, W.J. and Dunn, J.D. : Study of job satisfaction in six university libraries. *College and Research Libraries.* 35; May 1974. p. 163-177.
9. Wahva, S.P. : Job satisfaction of librarians; a comparison between men and women. *College and Research Libraries.* 36, January 1979. p. 45-51.
10. D'ehia, George P. : The determinants of job satisfaction among beginning librarians. *Library Quarterly.* 49(3), July 1979. p. 283-302.
11. Jones, N. and Jordan, P. : Op. cit., p. 32-33.
12. Luthans, F and Knod, E. : Critical factors in job enrichment. *Atlanta Economic Review.* May-June 1974.
13. Argyrgis, C. : Personal vs organisational goals. *Yole Scientific,* February 1960.
14. Plate K.H. and Stone, E.W. : Op. cit., p. 97.

Chapter 3

Library and its Working Group : A Study

The library, from its beginning is known as a social instrument. The formation of library presupposes the existence of a literature, whether it is preserved on clay tables, papyrus, parchment or paper. The earliest forms of libraries do not fit with our modern ideas and notions of the library because the form in which human records of knowledge have been recorded, were different from place to place and form time to time.

Modern ideas of libraries and library services have deep roots in the Middle Ages. The forms and services that can be found in 20th century libraries began to take shape in the early 17th century when older collections have been incorporated into permanent ones that have largely survived to the present and new collections. In the 17th, 18th and 19th centuries most of these collections developed independently. But in 20th century Government supported and academic, were formed that has forced rationalisation and integration of library services in all areas[1].

1. Library and the Concept of Organisational Module

The concept of organisational module has transformed to the library and different types of libraries have been established from 19th century. The great collections of renowned private libraries have been absorbed or replaced by old and new university libraries, by national libraries which furthered the new nationalism. Circulating and mercantile libraries have been established for the improvement of the workers, public libraries have been for the education and entertainment for adults, and special libraries have been established for the government bureaus, industrial concerns, historical studies and research. As the importance of libraries increased, or better to say, the importance of library has realised, the library became a complex organisation consisting of a conglomerate specialised activities.

Simon[2] has noticed this change and writes thus :

"In the early years of twentieth century, when the standard techniques and practices of library science were being worked out, the chief objective of libraries was that of building a scholarly collection without much thought for the people who the predominant objective in, or should be to provide the user with the information he needs not merely by calling upon the resources of the library where the request is made, but by tapping all the other resources that may be available elsewhere. This change in emphasis in the purpose of libraries, their growing size and diversification of activities, and their increase involvement with new technical methods and equipment - an involvement often requiring the addition of staff with specialised skills and knowledge - pose the question of a possible need for a new look at the organisational structure of libraries" (p.27).

2. Organisational Staff Position

While engaged in work in any organisation the staffs of that organisation are assigned different duties and responsibilities and the staffs of that organisation are performed that duties and responsibilities. On the basis of duties and responsibilities assigned to the staff and functions performed it is easily understandable that some members of staff are doing the managerial jobs and others are carrying orders from the managers and do their jobs. They are the common workers of the organisation. Therefore, there are two types of staff in any organisation : (1) Management staff and (2) Working staff.

Among the managers or management staff, the following classification has been adopted by the Executive Compensation Service of the American Management Association :

(*a*) Top management,

(*b*) Middle management,

(*c*) Supervisory management.

Top Management

This group of staff are responsible for the overall direction and success of the organisation. They are the policy making group. Top management group is a team of individuals at the highest level of organisational management. They hold excutive powers conferred on them by the appropriate authority of any organisation.

Middle Management

This group of staff are responsible for the execution of the policies and interpretation of policies throughout the organisation. This group of staffs may apply individual initiative and judgement for the successful operation of division or department assigned to them but act under policies and directives of top management.

Supervisory Management

This group of staff responsible for the final execution of policies by rank and file staffs. They are the point of direct contact with most staffs of that organisation. Supervisors are the key persons in management.[3] They make decisions, control work, interpret policy. They are the managements representative to the worker and worker's representative to the management.[4]

The above conception of staff position of organisation is well represented by Appleby[5] in the figure-1 of the organisational Pyramid.

3. The Library Management

The modern library is an organisation with a number of environments and its efficient functioning depends upon its ability to interact with those environments. There is a constant dynamic transfer and utilisation of organisational and environmental energy. Members of a library working group are reliant upon each other for the health and quality of the organisation. Service provided in libraries have become more active and exploitative as opposed to passive and custodial. In the context of this more dynamic approach to library organisation and function, there has been the need of adjustment and updating of policies and procedures. And this is the study of library management.

Modern library management is based on the science of administration and management as developed by Gulick and Urwick[6], Fayol[7] and others. These theories have been introduced into library administrative organisation by such librarian and writers as Wilson and Tauber[8], Rogers and Weber[9] and Thompson[10].

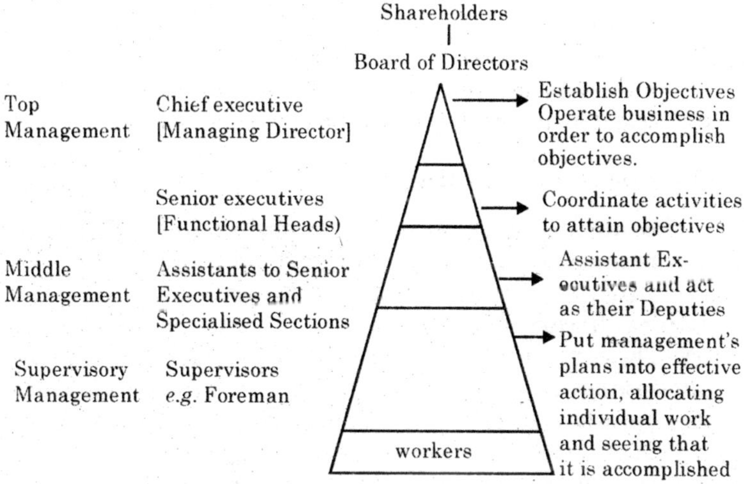

Figure 1 : Organisational Pyramid of an organisation.

4. Need for Group Studies in Libraries

Now, the libraries are established as unified systems. It has many sub-systems to fulfill its goal and objectives. It has all the opportunities of management activities including planning, organising, command, co-ordination and control. Therefore, group studies are essential for ever-growing library organisation.

5. Importance of Group Studies

Irrespective of their type and environment there are some common functions of a library that may be identified as :

(*a*) Administrative

(*b*) Personnel Management

(*c*) Public Relation

(*d*) Circulation

(*e*) Stock Selection (Book and non-book)

(*f*) Technical (manual and machine)

(*g*) Stock Control

(*h*) Financial

These above eight items are the broad categories of functions of libraries. Under these broad categories there are many pertinent task-areas existing in library organisations. On the basis of these functions of libraries group studies may be investigated in the field of Library Organisation.

6. Objective of the Study

Like any functional organisation library organisation has its own management system and style for its operation and proper functioning. To perform library operation and functioning, library staff are engaged in many task-areas in a library. The effectiveness of a library largely depends on how the different groups of library staff and the various task-areas are structurally and functionally integrated. The present study has considered the following aspects of components related to the library and group studies ingeneral, which may be shown in Table 1.

Actually, the major thrust of the present study has been to search group differentiation among the library staff and their levels in organisational structure.

6.1 Selection of Libraries

One the basis of objective of the study we have selected two University Libraries of West Bengal : (*a*) Burdwan University Library, P.O. and Dist. Burdwan and (*b*) Visva-Bharati university Library, P.O. Santiniketan, Dist. Birbhum. These University libraries are selected with the realisation that in our country University libraries are well-organised libraries and have normally all the divisions of modern libraries with a good number of staff.

Table 1 : Showing the Factors that have been Included in the Present Study

Component Related to Library		*Component related to Group Studies*	
Name	*Exact Factors*	*Differentiation*	*Factors*
Categories of staff	(*a*) Librarian	Groups of	(*a*) Top Management
	(*b*) Deputy Librarians	Library	(*b*) Middle Management
	(*c*) Assistant Librarians	Staffs	(*c*) Supervisory Management
	(*d*) Professional Assistants and its equivalent ranks		(*d*) Worker
	(*e*) Semi Professional Assistants and its equivalent ranks		

7. The Study

Organisation charts of the two libraries have been studied. From the organisation charts it has been realised that the following categories of staff are commonly associated with library organisations :

1. Librarians
2. Deputy Librarians
3. Assistant Librarians
4. Professional Assistants/Senior Technical Assistants or its equivalewnt ranks.
5. Semi Professional Assistants/Junior Technical Assistants or its equivalent ranks.
6. Library Attendants/Book Sorters
7. Office Staffs
8. Others

In the present study only five categories of library staff are included *viz.*, Librarians, Deputy Librarians, Assistant Librarians, Professional Assistants/Senior Technical Assistants and Semi Professional Assistants/Junior Technical Assistants. Almost all the staffs of Burdwan University Library and Visva-Bharati University Library have been covered under the study by distributing questionnaires. In the questionnaire the information needed to answer by the respondent are of two types :

1. Personal information about the respondent, and
2. Respondent's involvement with the library functioning.

After few days gap, the questionnaire has been collected from the respondents. The Table 2 will show the distribution and collection of questionnaire.

Table 2 : Distribution and Collection of Questionnaire

Name of the Library	*Questionnaire distributed to different categories of staff*	*Uncovered persons*	*Questionnaire collected from the respondents*	*Incomplete questionnaire received*	*Questionnaire actually studied*
B.U. Library	50	1	32	1	31
V.B.U. Library	53	2	35	2	33
Total	**103**	**3**	**67**	**3**	**64**

All the five staff categories are participants of this study. The total staff and the participants are shown in Table 3 :

Table 3 : Participation of Respondents of Two Libraries

Staff Categories	*B.U. Library*		*V.B.U. Library*	
	Actual	*Respondents*	*Actual*	*Respondents*
Librarian	1	1	1	1
Deputy Librarian	1	1	3	1
Asst. Librarian	4	3	9	6
Professional Asstt./ Sr. Technical Asstt./ equivalents	21	13	20	18
Semi Professional Asstt./Jr. Technical Asstt./equivalents	24	13	24	7
Total	51	31	57	33

From the two tables it appears that total 103 questionnaires have been distributed in two libraries and only three staff reamin uncovered. Altogether 67 questionnaires have been collected from the respondants, but 3 remains incomplete. So this study considers 64 questionnaires out of which Burdwan University Library respondents are 31 and Visva Bharati University Library respondants are 33.

8. Analysis

To analyse the questionnaire the following matter has been considered :

1. Identification of the library.
2. Identification of staff category.
3. Identification of job involvement regarding library function and operation as mentioned in item 5 of this study.

After analysing the questionnaire from the respondents it is evident that both the libraries have five categories of staff. All the eight types of library functions and operations (as mentioned in item No. 5) are performed in both the libraries. On the basis of the analysis of the two libraries, Visva-Bharati University Library and Burdwan University Library a scheme for the working group of library staff has determined and shown in Figure 2.

Although the scheme is self-explanatory, it needs little clarification. It may be noted that in the scheme, five categories of employees of library organisation *i.e.*, Librarians, Deputy Librarians, Professional Assistant and its equivalent ranks, and Semi-Professional Assistant and its equivalent ranks have been included. One question may be asked, why certain categories have been included in two alternative groups? Study into the organisational chart of different libraries has led to outline the scheme. The Librarian, Deputy Librarian and Assistant Librarians belong to management group. Professional Assistant and its equivalent ranks belong to supervisory group, and Semi-Professional Assistant and its equivalent ranks belong to working group. These groupings are permanents in library organisation which are represented by line boxes.

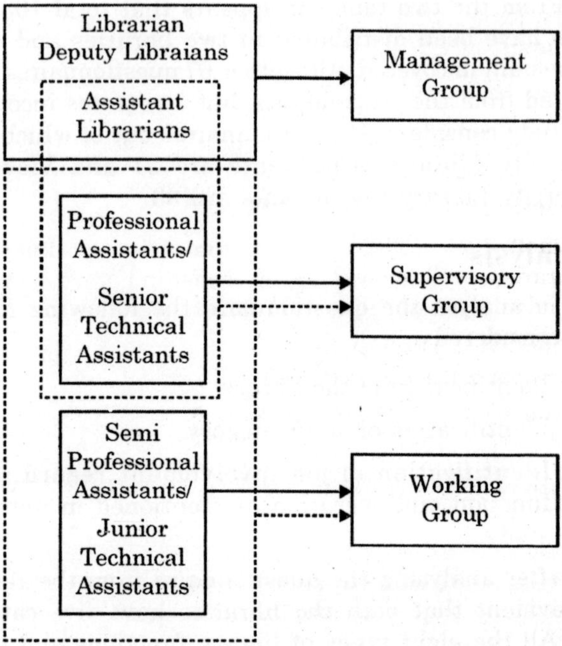

Figure 2 : Schematic presentation of Working Groups of Library Organisation.

Simultaneously, the operations and functioning of different libraries have been studied where these groupings are flexible and conjoined different categories into the same group, which are represented by dotted boxes. In library organisations Assistant Librarians belong to management group as well as supervisory group, and Professional Assistant and its equivalent ranks belong to supervisory group as well as working group, depending upon the exact duties they are assigned with.

9. Conclusion

On the basis of the above analysis, though it is based on the study of only two libraries, the Visva-Bharati University Library and Burdwan University Library, it is an attempt to determine the scheme for library working group in existence.

It is believed that this schematic pattern of library working group exists throughout the Indian Library

Organisations with a slight variation depending upon the local environment of the library.

References

1. Thompson, L.S. : History of libraries : from 1600 to World War II. *In* The Encyclopedia Americana, Vol, 17. New York: Americana Corporation, 1976.
2. Simon, B.V. : The need for administrative know-how in libraries. *In* Shimon, R. ed. : A reader in library management, London : Bigley, 1976. p. 17-34.
3. Devis, K. : Human Behaviour a work : Organisational behaviour. 6th ed. New Delhi : Tata McGrew-Hill, 1981.
4. Banerjee, M. : Gems of Management. Calcutta : Jaico Publishing, 1986.
5. Appleby, R.C. : Modern Business Administration. London : Pitman, 1969.
6. Gulick L.H. and Urwick, L. eds. : Papers on the science of administration. New York : Institute of Public Administration, Colombia University, 1937.
7. Fayol, H. : General and industrial management, trans. by Constance Storrs. London : Pitman, 1949. (Original in French. 1916).
8. Wilson, L.R. and Tauber, M.P. : The University Library : the organisation, administration and formation of modern academic libraries. 2nd ed. New York : Colombia Univ., 1956.
9. Roger, R.D. and Weber, D.C. : University Library administration. New York : Wilson, 1971.
10. Thompson, J. : An introduction to University library administration. 3rd. ed. London : Bigley, 1979.

Chapter 4

Library Profession and its Code of Ethics

The emergence of code of ethics for library profession is perhaps the most important in the context of the recent library development of our country. It is admitted that the success of a profession depends on the charter or by an act of the legislature. At present, in India seventeen States declared their library laws. Library Directorates are created in these seventeen States. Movement for National Library Policy is patronized by the Central Government. This is a good symbol for the practicing librarians to claim the library occupation as a 'profession' like the other 'law profession', 'medical profession', etc.

1. Conceptualizing Profession

Before we proceed, let us clarify about the term profession. Professions developed in the historical process in response to specific social context and they created reality which become part of the social context. In the first part of 19th century, scientific development and extension of modernisation grown through industrialisation and technological progress. The ideology of 'status professionalism' was gradually transformed into 'occupational professionalism' during this periodicity. During this period, medicine, law, engineering, teaching, journalism, nursing has grown as modern professions and also the professional institutions have been established and more closely linked with work, labour, and social satisfaction.

2. Definition

It is very difficult to offer a definition of 'profession' which will be accepted by all with full satisfaction. The concept of 'profession' has a varity of meaning. The dictionary fails to provide a definition which is unanimously accepted by all. Again, synonymously, the term 'profession' is frequently used as 'occupation'.

Oxford English Dictionary[1] defines the term profession as "A vocation in which a professed knowledged of some department of learning or science is used in its application to the affairs of others or in the practice of an art founded upon it."

Here the dictionary definition lays emphasis on intellectualistic dimension of profession only, but it ignores the ethical and authority aspects.

Dictionary of Soical Sciences[2] puts it thus :

"The term profession denotes occupations which demand a highly specialized knowledge and skill acquired at least in part by courses of a more or less theoretical nature and not by practice alone, tested by some from of examination either at a universtiy or some other authorised instisution, and conveying to the persons who possess them considerable authority in relation to 'clients'."

Here, in this definition, social aspects of professions are stressed on but it ignores the individual aspect .

It is clear that none of these definitions alone convey the concept of 'profession' in a complete sense. To avoid this difficulty, scholars tried to define 'profession' by criteria. According to Carr-Saunders[3], 'A profession may be defined as an occupation based upon specialized intellectual study and training, the purpose of which is to supply skilled service or adivce to others for a definite fee or salary".

Greenwood[4] has attempted to distinguish profession from the non-professions in terms of five elements. These elements are : (*i*) systematic theory, (*ii*) authority, (*iii*) community sanction, (*iv*) ethical code, and (*v*) a culture. These five elements or attributes were reviewed by Greenwood after two decades of writing his earlier paper. Now after revision, he has recognised three attributes of profession, *viz.* (*a*) cognitive, (*b*) normative and (*c*) monopolistic attributed. He has argued that his persent conceptualization and terminology is much more accurate and clear in replacing the term as choosed earlier *i.e,* systematic theory, ethical codes and community sanction respectively. He also argues that the other two elements or attributes as accepted earlier (authority/autonomy and culture) are the derivatives. From the combination of all the basic components, as accepted now, are derived.[5]

Maclver[6] identifies the essential characteristies of profession as : (*a*) the ideal of service (*b*) an ethical code, and (*c*) the welfare of society. When a profession established in a society or the pattern in which occupations have own professional recognition it has the following six steps :

(*i*) the occupation requires a full time to its members;

(*ii*) formal training is initiated;

(*iii*) training is recognised within universities;

(*iv*) national and local associations are formed;

(*v*) a code of ethics is adopted; and

(*vi*) licensing and certifications are established[7].

In each profession, there is a functional relevency either for the society as a whole or for the individual client as a social being. The function is performed by the well trained practitioners who dare for their personal profit.

3. Is Librarianship a Profession?

Dr. S.R. Ranganathnan[8], the father of librarianship in India, has stated that the librarianship is a profession because it possesses all the traditional attributes of the professionalism. There is no doubt to declare the librianship as profession as it has the following characteristics :

(*a*) Librarians' jobs are service oriented and not profit oriented;

(*b*) It is a systematic as well as general branch of knowledge;

(*c*) Universities and other Institutes facilitates the teaching courses, *e.g.* Certificate, B.L.I.S., M.L.I.S., Associateship, Ph.D., etc. After receiving these degrees only people have the chance to enter the librarianship.

(*d*) Librarianship has established as a full-time occuption;

(*e*) It serves its clientele adequately;

(*f*) The government has a full support to this occuption. In India, seventeen States have already declared Library Law. Library Directorates are created in these States. And, the States where this law is lacking, political agitation is directed for the establishment of this law;

(*g*) Librarianship has the professional status;

(*h*) It has established the national and local professional associations and that associations are orgainsed and controlled by the librarians, the working specialists themselves; and

(*i*) These professional associations have taken steps to register the code of ethics for the librarianship.

4. Code of Ethics

Code of ethics, in any profession, based on ethical point of view which compels to maintain some ethical behaviour among its members. It makes the profession's commitment to social services as a matter of public record. Code of ethics are voluntary in nature and that are partly formal or in the written form and partly informal or in unwritten form. It has some regulative measures. It mainly regulates ethical behaviours of clientele-professional relations and colleague-colleague relations. Code of ethics are vatried among professions but it is essential to each profession. Normally, professional associations sketch this code of ethics. To each and every professional person, it is a high degree of self control behavior which iternalised in the process of work socialization. The context of the efficiency of codes of ethics depend upon mutual understanding and common interest of the professional groups.

5. Code of Ethics for Library Profession

Standard library service depends upon the quality of the individual practicing librarian and this reflects the whole profession. The library profession should, therefore, register its code of ethics which exercise more responsibility to the individuals and group of library practitioners. The codes of ethics for the library profession may be as under :

5.1 Responsibility to Users

(*a*) Clientele are same irrespective of caste, creed, sex and status.

(*b*) Adequate and quick service to the clientele.

(*c*) Attend each client though the client may left the library with no choice.

(*d*) Arrangement of user education programme or orientation programme.

5.2 Responsibility to Authority

(*a*) Realise the authority expectation.

(*b*) Take initiative to perform the organisational tasks.

(*c*) Try to achieve a healthy balance between the aims of the employee and the aims of the employer, the reciprocal relationship.

5.3 Responsibility to Coleagues and Other Institution Librarians

(*a*) Provide staff development programme.

(*b*) Create joint and co-operative relationship with the colleagues and other subordinates to achieve the highest goal, purpose and objective of the library.

(*c*) Create such relationship between employee and the library for which colleagues and subordinates are willing to expend energy on the library tasks.

(*d*) Librarians of different institutes co-operate more meaningfully among themselves to expand co-ordinative leadership in community development.

5.4 Administrative Responsibilities

(*a*) Sketch organisational design which ensures employee to realise their expectation at work.

(*b*) Motivate employee to gain the objectives of the concerned library in its highest degree.

(*c*) Make himself a good leader.

(*d*) Should be unbiased in case of taking any administrative decision.

(*e*) Adopt democratic and participative management style for the proper functioning of the library.

(*f*) Provide upward, downward and sideward communication processes which obviously help to overcome any problem occured in the service points of the library.

5.5 Responsibility to Property and Finance

(*a*) Think document/material of the library as personal.

(*b*) Keep maintenance of the documents, and other library materials.

(*c*) Prepare library budget.

(*d*) Take effective steps in favour of cost effectiveness.

5.6 Self Enrichment

(*a*) Self study; for improving, developing, deepening and refreshing own knowledge and skill.

(*b*) Continuing education; which means to attend conferences and seminars organised by different Library Associations, Library Teaching Institutes or individual Library Organisations which have Regional, State or National constituencies.

The above are helpful processes for self enrichment. Those are also helpful for the future development of the individual library organisation and the library profession as a whole.

5.7 Responsibility to Develop Library Profession

(*a*) Integrate the library organisation with the society by providing (1) standard, (2) quickest and (3) adequate services.

(*b*) Realize the concept that the library services are for the total community development and, therefore, it is necessary : (*i*) to promote continuous study and review the community, (*ii*) to identify the informational and educational needs and interest of the community, and (*iii*) to provide informational programme to meet such needs and interests of the community.

5.8 Responsibility to Develop Education

(*a*) Recommend/suggest for future development of the library education.

(*b*) Provide extension lectures in different library education institutes,

The librarians have all the above eight field of responsibilities in the library profession. Code of ethics must be broad in nature and it acts as a guideline for the working librarians. Therefore, the competent authority, before to prepare the code of ethics for the library profession should keep in mind for the field of responsibilities of the librarians as mentioned above.

6. Conclusion

From the above discussion we may conclude that code of ethics is must for the library profession. Now the question naturally may come that who will take the responsibility to prepare the code of ethics for the library profession? And the answer for the question will be the library association should shoulder the responsibilities for the preparation of code of ethics for the noble profession. It is true that library associations such as IASLIC, ILA, IATLIS etc. have taken some steps to formulate the code of ethics for Indian Librarians. But those movements are not enough/sound actions, likely required for the current changing situations or realities of digital environment taking place in Indian libraries.

The initiation to form library association generally came from the most skilled, competent and distinguished practicing librarians with a view to keeping charlatans out and securing the library profession a respectable status in society. The chief function of library association may be to keep pace with the constant continuous advancement of modern library science education and service, and make rooms to acquire the advance knowledge for each and every member of this profession by which they identify themselves most competent for the changing situation. The other vital functions of the library associations may be as under.

(*a*). To organise the group of library professionals to create a true library culture among the symmetrical libraries.

(*b*) To define standards of competence.

(c) To control entry into the library profession through proper influence on library education, and

(*d*) To define standard of ethical conduct for the profession.

References

1. (The) Oxford English Dictionary VIII. Oxford : Clarendon Press, 1933. p. 1427.
2. Elias, N. : Professions. *In* A dictionary of the social sciences, edited by Gould, J. and Kolb, W.L., compiled under the auspices of the UNESCO. New York : Free Press, 1964. p. 542.
3. Carr-Saunder, A.M. : Profession : their organisation and place in society. Oxford : Clarendon Press, 1928. p. 4.
4. Greenwood, E. : Attributes of a profession. *Social Work* : 1957, 2(3), p. 44-45.
5. Greenwood, E.: Attributes of a profession : revisited. *In* Lat, S.K. and others (eds.) : Readings in the sociology of the profession. Delhi : Gian Publisghing, 1988, p. 3-29.
6. Maclver, R. : Social significance of professional ethics. *The Annals of American Academy of Political and Social Science*. 1955, 297. p. 118-124.
7. Johnson,T.J. : Profession and power. New York : Macmillan, 1972.
8. Ranganathan, S.R. : Is there a library profession? *Library Herald*. 1968, 10. p. 105-110.

Chapter 5

Changing Dimensions of Library and Information Services in E-Library Environment

The present era is the information era and we have our 'right to information' by law. Central Government of India placed one bill of Right to Information in its Parliament and finallv, the Indian Parliament passed the Act. This Act is named as the Right to Information Act, 2005. Subject to the provisions of this Act, all citizens of India shall have the right to information[1].

The mission of library service is to support the purposes of the group to be served with their needed information. The role of library service is to provide access to documents, which generously include a range of informative objects that can be stored and retrieved, not only writings and not only published writings.

Library services are concerned with texts and images that are representations of knowledge. Library services are, in practice, often concerned less with the texts and images themselves than with physical objects that are text-bearing and image-bearing, such as books, journals, manuscripts, and photographs. Libraries deal with text-bearing and image-bearing objects in vast quantities. Much of libraries' operating budgets and space is devoted not to the *use* of these materials, but to the *assembling, organizing, and describing* them so that it would become possible to use them as and when required. Hence, any significant change in the technology of text-bearing objects or of handling them could have very profound consequences, not on the purpose and mission of library services, but on the means for achieving them.

1. Basic Information Needs of People

In the light of Right to Information Act, the people of India should have the wider scope of gathering information on different aspects of life and the facilities offered and maintained by the Central and State Governments. This information support is essential for rural and urban people for four basics: socio-economic, technological, industrial and political development; and detail areas of these are :

"(*a*) *Resource Data* : In terms of land use, cropping area, water bodies and drainage, soil and mineral resources.

(*b*) *Demographic Data* : Relating to population, sex ratio, age structure, urban and rural population, schedule caste and schedule tribe population, occupational structure, migration, etc.

(*c*) *Agro-Economic Data* : Comprising information about cropped and irrigated area, agricultural production, land holdings, live stock populations, etc.

(*d*) Socio-Economic Activities : Relating to industrial, fishing activities, tourism development as well as beneficiary of various schemes and programmes for development.

(*e*) Infrastructure Data : Relating to availability and level of various facilities, utilities and services such as education, health, power, transport, network, water supply, drainage, etc.

All the above information can be stored in the form of text, sound, picture, video and other media forms that can be transferred, shared and accessed by the people throughout country and globally and for this, the establishment of infrastructure is an imperative for the future of the society, calling upon us to address associated issues of networks, communications, databases, spatial information systems, and advanced applications"[2].

Depending on the soundness of Information System, the country moves ahead for its total development. We have some communication networks and information databases all through out the country, but the people of village areas are too poor and out of reach of these information. Public Library can be linked to this information system and thus rural people will be benefited and enlighten on the latest developments in the area of agriculture, crop insurance and marketing, traditional and alternative cultivations, rural cottage industries, fisheries and animal husbandry, small business, finances from banks and other sources, panchayeti-raj, etc.

2. Basic Information Needs of University People

Again, the need for education and research of any university is always highly dependant on latest information of a subject study or allied disciplines. University education requires well established library of its own with sound collection of subjects studied in that particular higher learning institute. But it is impossible to procure all the necessary documents/data/information even for any single subject in any university as the growth of information/publication in any subject is growing on very high speed. In view of the development of Information and Communication Technology (ICT) the users of university library are fond of recent development in his/her topic of research/interest. They place demands for the required document/data/information that is not available to parent institute library with the intention that library should procure those on behalf of them to avoid delay and hardship. A new trend now appears which claims the library should be committed to provide access only. The meaning of access now reveals not access to one's collection but access to the entire world of materials *i.e.* entire data/information/knowledge world.

3. Need for Developing Environment in Library

Therefore, it necessitates to develop the new environment in any library where users need and demand for new knowledge could be provided, which are generated anywhere in the world. And if the library under go with this new system another development automatically be established, the librarian will always be ready to serve the clientele of the organization plus other persons through out the world.

To face the demands of users, librarians have to introduce automation, a new environment to his/her library. Librarian has to take initiative to serve his/her clientele in two ways :

1. from the internal resources of the library and
2. from the external resources. Librarian is also interested to serve outsiders those are not the members of the library.

By providing this service librarian should take initiative to build this new environment to his/ her library with necessary fund provision for Library Automation and introduction of ICT. Thus, Electronic Library establishes which helps to remove many of the constraints of the Paper Library, such as the effective limitation to local collections, the tendency for desired books to be unavailable, limited opening hours, and, especially, the need to go to the library in order to use it.

Presently, ICT is deeply influencing the librarian in respect of how data/information/knowledge is to be acquired, organized, stored, retrieved and disseminated; how library services and facilities are to be designed, organized, staffed and offered; and how the library users seek, receive and use their required data/information/knowledge. The new tools provide powerful options for working with data, text, sound, and images.

4. Changing Situations : On Library Part

The change from the Traditional Library to Digital Library has been primarily a matter of computerizing the library's internal procedures. The first change is creation of on-line catalog to replace the card catalog. The on-line catalog has two quite kinds of impact. For all who visit the library it is a different sort of catalog, with a keyboard, screen, and a new way of searching to be learned in the place of passive trays of cards.

Secondly, the library will now be able to provide access from *within* the library from the in-house materials stored electronically and to generate copies on paper, which is clearly a useful extension of service.

Thirdly, the library will now be able to arrange for access from *outside* the library materials, stored electronically elsewhere in the world, by surfing Website in such a way that users with suitable equipment and skills can use these resources by themselves, which constitutes a much more substantial extension of library service.

Fourthly, the shift from the Traditional Library to Digital Library ensures the provision of printouts of the results of bibliographic searches performed by librarians for library users.

With the Digital Library, much more service is possible in expanded use of library service, which will facilitate self-service than one-on-one service by library staff, even though the latter will remain necessary and desirable and even though the tasks facing the library users are becoming more complex.

5. Changing Situations : on Readers'/ Users' Part

The Digital Library will be useful but the benefits are not fully achieved until the library users work electronically. This Library has to change among library users' working habits. The impact will go to library users, as the users have to notice computerized catalogue in place of card catalogue, improved circulation procedures and better-produced lists of various kinds.

A different impact has been on the growing proportion of library users whose work habits and working environment have changed for inclusion of computers even in library routine use. For these people the option of remote access to the library's catalog has constituted an important new extension of library service. It is an enhancement of service primarily for those who have work habits with the new equipment.

A strategic shift from the direct provision of service one-on-one to the design and provision of library services intended for self-service seems inevitable, even though library services are becoming more powerful and more complex. One-on-one service by library staff will remain necessary and desirable for getting self-service, at least in the preliminary stages of its introduction and also for the new users, in the changing situation browsing for information through electronic media as the tasks facing the library users are becoming more complex.

6. Changing in the Library Environment

Extensive use of the Digital Library depends on a change

in the work habits and working environment of library users. The fact is that this enhancement of service through the automation of the catalog is of benefit only to those who had the technology to use it. In many work environments, especially in universities and corporations; among professionals, administrative, employees and writers; generally we find widespread and increasing use of computers and telecommunications. People who have moved to a personal computing environment for their work they *need* the provision of a Digital Library because the effective conduct of their work is based on access to electronic records.

In contrast, the new information technology is transforming the use of library materials, with computer-based techniques for identifying, locating, accessing, transferring, analyzing, manipulating, comparing, and revising texts, images, sounds, and data.

7. Expected Library Services in Changing Environment

It is expected, on starting point of library services, the principle would be that those who now use the new information technology should make the kinds of services provided in the Traditional Library, available for use. Hence from a computer anywhere a library user should be able :

1. To search the library catalog, including all cataloged holdings, without need to refer to additional catalogs on card or on microfiche. The library "catalog" is best seen as a series of concentric circles that include the holdings of the local library, of nearby, and of distant libraries. Within each catalog category, the searcher should have the option of expanding a search to associated files: circulation records, incompletely cataloged materials, and files of materials that are on order.
2. To search in bibliographies and also to be able to find the items listed, whether on paper, on microform, or on-line.
3. To search in directories and reference works.

4. To search for numeric data in social, technical, economic, and scientific databases—and to retrieve conveniently whichever datasets are needed.
5. To search for images and moving images—pictures currently on slides, movies, photos, videotapes—and to retrieve copies for use.
6. To search for texts, whether texts that were already known or those discovered in a catalog or bibliography.

These resources (catalogs, bibliographies, directories, numerical data, images, and texts) should be available for library users at their place of work using the tools with which they normally work, which implies copying in electronic form into personal storage, printing, or ordering a copy of printed material. These resources should suit the user's convenience by being available when needed, requiring minimal effort or formality, blend smoothly with personal computing practices. They should allow for convenient movement from one file or function to another and for integration of computerized with non-automated procedures.

7.1 : Self-Service

Difficulties arise both because library users' needs are so extensive and so varied and because the sources of information are too complex, too imperfect, and too incomplete for self-service to be adequate. It is inherently unreasonable to assume that the provision of unaided library "self-service" will be satisfactory.

7.2 : Assistance Service

Assistance is needed of three overlapping kinds : reference service, library instruction, and referral. These different sorts of responses are not mutually exclusive. Which, or which combination, would be most cost-effective in any given case may vary greatly. The library's first significant task, from the standpoint of the user, is to help with the identification and location of needed material. For many types of materials, the bibliographic tools available for this task are complex or incomplete, and the user is unlikely to be successful in finding the material needed without help. Librarians are therefore needed to assist users in interpreting such tools, and to ensure that all suitable possible sources of information are made known to the reader.

The advent of computerized services for searching machine-readable data bases has also added a new dimension to reference and information services. Many of the major abstracting and indexing services, such as *Chemical Abstracts* and the *Readers' Guide*, are now searched on-line as well as on paper. Increasingly bibliographies are available not only from on-line search services but also as optical digital disks (CD-ROMs) that can be searched inside the library and as files mounted on on-line library catalogs. The commands to use these systems differ and the on-line version may not be the same as the paper version where both exist.

7.3 : Instruction Service

There are various ways in which instruction in using libraries can be given. At the simplest level it is "orientation", a technique or guided tour and the main purpose of which is to familiarize students with the layout of the library building and the location of various resources and services.

At a more specific level, there are also "point-of-use" instructions, including printed guides on basic techniques in using the resources of the library; brochures on how to use bibliographic tools, such as indexing and abstracting services; video-tape, audio tape and slide-tape presentations; and personal guidance by reference librarians in methods of pursuing research in particular fields.

A third type of instruction has also gained increasing support in academic libraries: the formal course in bibliographic and research methods, offered for academic credit, and particularly designed for undergraduate students. The major objective of such classes is to impart skills for continuing self-education on the part of the student. Library instruction can be expensive and labor-intensive, but the prospect of a major increase in self-service makes it an important and a more plausible investment. Library service can be characterized by reaching out successful users to teach them

7.4 : Referral Services

The other form of assistance is referral to other sources. This might be a difficult question being referred to another, more specialized library, librarian, or other expert or referring a library user to another more appropriate source. In both cases it is necessary to know to whom or to where a referral can be made with a reasonable chance of success. The development of detailed knowledge of resources is necessary for referral to work effectively.

Library use and bibliographic research are complex and becoming more so. A greater investment in user education will be needed to ensure that effective use is made of library resources, all the more so as any library's resources comes to include the resources of all cooperating libraries. Such an investment is needed if library users are to achieve a return on the greater investment in the creation of Paper, Automated, and Electronic Libraries[3].

8. Drives for the Success of the Programme

For creation of new digital or electronic library environment and its smooth operation library planners, librarians, professional bodies, Government bodies and Non-government organizations should come forward. As it is the necessity of the society, joint venture is required and it is beyond sole control of librarians. In the new environment, there is increasing complexity, problems arise when the user's expertise is inadequate for the task. Different sorts of response are possible :

1. ***User Education :*** Expertise can be increased.
2. ***Advice :*** The system could possibly be designed to offer helpful guidance or prompts.
3. ***Simplification :*** If the complexity facing the user could be reduced, then the user's expertise would become more adequate *relative to* the task.
4. ***Mediation :*** Providing an expert human intermediary to provide assistance—a reference librarian, for example—is an obvious course of action.

5. ***Delegation :*** It may be possible to shift some of the task complexity inside the system. Make the system itself smarter, more capable of determining what should be done next.

In real situation it is found that Electronic Library involves with a heterogeneous hardware and software environment that requires a heavy emphasis on compatibility, linking, and interoperability through standardized protocols.

The substitution of computing power, electronic data storage, and use of telecommunications holds considerable potential, not least because of the expectation that they will continue to become more attractive on cost grounds. The important questions become how and when the substitution of procedures based on new information technology should be adopted. A large amount of funding is indispensable to initiate the Digital Library programme in an individual library and cluster of libraries situated through out the country. It may be just noted that in the provision of library service a very large proportion of present budgets is devoted for arranging the means to enable service to be provided. Digital Library has an attempt for ever-increasing proportion of the use of library services from outside the library, even from remote areas of a country or globally. Information communication technology may only be a means and not an end; there should be provision for a corresponding increase in library staffing sound with information technology skill to make a success of the programme.

9. Some Constrains

The constraints include our limited ability to determine how to achieve that substitution, when that substitution will become cost-effective, and, at least as important, how to discriminate between substitutions that support improved library service and substitutions that subverts the mission and role of library service. The initial task can reasonably be to find out how and when to substitute techniques using new information technology in the place of more traditional methods. Sometimes it misjudges the real options. Each technology offers a different set of constraints. Each technology is suitable for doing different things. The automating of manual procedures may well be worthwhile, but may create problem in the long run at the point of technological change.

10. Conclusion

The main task of library services for the past, present and in future is to help users and to meet their needs. Librarians have done the job very well in the past. But, recent years the characteristics and needs of library users are constantly changing in response to social changes, with integration of new equipment and technology of ICT in the field of Library and Information Science. For the inclusion of specialized tools, increasing integration of technologies and use of networking, the library management and professionals are facing some kind of hardship, which is more dependency to the outside specialists or technicians. Library service is a value added service to the client of the library. The best library service combines information seeking, guidance and instruction. It also includes lessons in analysis and evaluation of the value of the information retrieved and the accuracy or correctness of the method of retrieval.

Present day librarians thus face both opportunities and challenges. They are constantly trying to find new and better ways of providing appropriate information, guidance and instruction to the user community they serve. In a changing world, this is not easy, but this goal of library services is unchanging. For successful library operation and providing library services, it is essential for improvement of skills of library professionals and it is a continuous process in library like other organizations.

References

1. http://persmin.nic.in/RTI/WelcomeRTI.htm.
2. Kasturirangan, K. and Rao, D.P. : Urban planning and management: space technology options. *In* Sikdar, P.K. Dhingra, S.L. and Rao, K.V.K. : Computers in urban planning and urban management: keynote papers. New Delhi: Narosa Publishing, 1998. p. 50-58.
3. Buckland, Michael K. and Florian, Doris : Expertise, task complexity, and artificial intelligence: a conceptual framework. *Journal of the American Society for Information Science.* 42 (1991). p. 635-643.

Chapter 6

Open Source Softwares and Their Applications in Libraries

Open source software has created an increasingly high profile in the field of library and information science management profession since 1999. It was due to an assemblage of 80 senior American academic library managers. In that meeting, three "keystone principles" were accepted to set a foundation for future developments of library services.

"The Keystone Principles invoke and express the urgency of three areas requiring explicit action based on a vivid set of user-centered principles". Out of these, principal two was regarding 'Open software', which stated the matter as: "libraries are responsible for creating innovative information systems for the dissemination and preservation of information and new knowledge regardless of format". It had an action item for libraries that to "create interoperability in the systems they develop and create open source software for the access, dissemination, and management of information"[1].

Members of the library and information science professionals continued this discussion to have a high level of interest in respect of open source software and for that over 200 articles and conference papers were published on describing specific library projects during four years after the first meeting held on September 1999.

1. Open Source Software : the Concept

Open source generally refers to a program where source code is available to the general public for their use and/or modification from its original design without paying any charge for that. Open source code is typically created as a collaborative effort in which programmers improve upon the code and share the changes within the community. Open source software helps programmers on the Internet read, redistribute and modify the source code, forcing an expedient evolution of the product. The process of eliminating bugs and improving the software happens at a much quicker rate than through the traditional development channels of commercial software as the information is shared throughout the open source community. Thus uses of open source software in various applications have been increased at a very high rate. The application field of library and information science has no exception of it[2].

2. Open Source Software: Definition

One website defines 'Open Source' as: "Open source promotes software reliability and quality by supporting independent peer review and rapid evaluation of source code. To be certified as open source, the license of a program must guarantee the right to read, redistribute, modify, and use it freely"[3].

According to International Encyclopedia of Information and Library Science "Open source software is available free of charge, and includes both the source code and the compiled version. Developers who accept the open source concept believe that software is a common good that should be shared rather than sold or profit, and that it can best be adapted, improved and re-bugged by its users. To make this possible the users need access to the source code"[4].

Dictionary for Library and Information Science defines Open source as : "A computer program for which the source code is made available without charge by the owner or licenser, usually via the Internet, to encourage the rapid development of a more useful and bug-free product through open peer review. The practice also allows the product to be customized by its users to suit local needs (example: Linux operating system). To be certified "open source" under the Open Source Initiative (OSI), software must meet certain established criteria that include no restrictions on access"[5].

3. Open Source Software: Certification

A certification standard issued by the Open Source

Initiative (OSI) that indicates that the source code of a computer program is made available free of charge to the general public. The rationale for this movement is that a larger group of programmers not concerned with proprietary ownership or financial gain will produce a more useful and bug-free product for everyone to use. OSI dictates that in order to be considered "OSI Certified" a product must meet the following criteria :

- The author or holder of the license of the source code cannot collect royalties on the distribution of the program.
- The distributed program must make the source code accessible to the user.
- The author must allow modifications and derivations of the work under the program's original name.
- No person, group or field of endeavor can be denied access to the program.
- The rights attached to the program must not depend on the program's being part of a particular software distribution.
- The licensed software cannot place restrictions on other software that is distributed with it.

4. Open Source Software: Salient Features

It has been realized from the above discussion that the Open Source Software has some special features. Dipen Deka[6] has also identified these special features as under :

- Open Source Software is normally created and maintained by developers crossing institutional and national boundaries, collaborating by using internet-based communications and development tools.
- Products are typically a kind of "free", often through a license that specifies that applications and source code are free to use, modify, and redistribute as long as all uses, modifications, and redistributions are similarly licensed.
- Successful applications are tend to be developed more quickly and with better responsiveness to the needs of

users who can readily use and evaluate open source applications because they are free.

- Quality, not profit drives the open source developers who take personal pride in seeing their working solutions adopted.
- Intellectual property rights to open software belong to everyone who helps to built it or simply uses it, not just the vendor or institution that creator of the software.

5. Open Source Software: Users Rights

The 'Open Source Software' by definition is a 'bill of rights' for the computer user. Programs like the *Linux* operating system and Netscape's web browser have become extremely popular, displacing other software with more restrictive licenses. Several companies that use Open Source software have the advantage of its very rapid development, often by several collaborating companies, and much of it contributed by individuals who simply need an improvement to serve their own needs. Programmers feel comfortable contributing to Open Source because they are assured of these rights :

- The right to make copies of the program, and distribute those copies.
- The right to have access to the software's source code, a necessary preliminary before you can change it.
- The right to make improvements to the program.

6. Open Source Software: Library Usage

Libraries in India like other parts of the world having used Open Software for several purposes: for house keeping, content creation, managerial functioning, etc. Libraries are using these only for their great advantages. Some of the advantages are :

- Start-up cost is very low, which attracts librarians for introduction of IT applications to different libraries.
- Open Software licenses mean that software can be run on multiple machines (or at home or on laptops) with no extra licensing fees. So it is beneficial for the intranet library operations and uses.

- Open Software acts as quick problem solver mechanism by exploiting many libraries experience in comparison with commercial integrated library system software, which is very slower to develop and expensive to upgrade.
- Open Software includes more flexibility and thus has a better match to libraries' requirements.
- Open Software has need-driven development process, where as commercial software has market driven process.[7]

Like different service organizations Open Source Software are available for libraries. Currently available Open Source Software library-related applications, which include not only integrated library management systems but also include a wide range of innovative functionalities, such as : data capturing, storing, indexing, preserving, distributing, etc. Some of the popular library Open Source Software has already been identified as :

(*a*) D Space,

(*b*) Greenstone,

(*c*) Koha,

(*d*) MyLibrary,

(*e*) Avanti,

(*f*) Eprints, etc.

6.1 : Indian Scenario

Open Source Software has increasingly been popularized in Indian libraries. Some of higher educational institute libraries and information centers have extensively using different Open Source Software for managing their libraries. Indian libraries have also used this Open Source Software for building up their digital libraries. The DSpace software has been used by DRTC, ISI, Bangalore; IIT, Delhi; INFLIBNET, Ahmedabad; National Chemical Laboratory; NIT, Rourkela; IIT, Kharagpur, etc. The Greenstone software has been used in IIT, Bombay library. The IISC, Bangalore and National Informatics Centre have been used the Eprint software. The software is used by Vidyasagar University on trial basis.

6.2 : Open Source Software and Visva-Bharati Library

Visva-Bharati Library is now using Open Source Software LINUX Red Hat as operating system and also using proprietary Software Libsys 4 (Unicode) for the management of its library system. Visva-Bharati Library is also using Avro open source software for transcription of Bengali interface in this particular proprietary software Libsys 4 (Unicode). The Library is taking regular updating for using Avro open source software, which helps much in respect of library housekeeping and operation. The Visva-Bharati Library has now been using both the proprietary and open software in combined form very well and thus three modules *i.e.* Cataloguing, Circulation and OPAC of the Libsys 4 (Unicode) software have been functioning successfully. The following figure will show this combined use of open source software and proprietary software at Visva-Bharati Library.

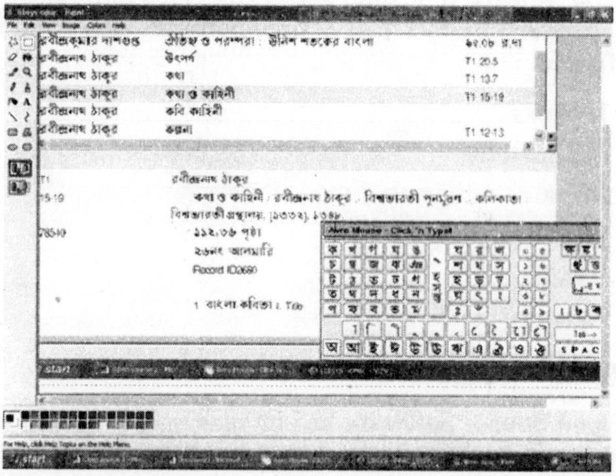

Figure 1 : Use of Open Source Software and Proprietary Software (in combined form) at Visva-Bharati Library.

Visva-Bharati Library is using My SQL and PHP, which are open source software by nature. This software are using for metadata search and full-text e-content access, which are actually created by the library from its "own content." The library is also using open source software 'Webalizer' for usage analysis of library's website.

7. Conclusion

Some debates exist for and against in respect of Open Source Software applications in different organizations. Some opine that there is a risk to use Open Source Software even though the initial cost is zero, supporting the software over its lifetime may involve considerable costs, and organisations may find it difficult to estimate these costs when the software is initially adopted. Again, in case where more control over the software is necessary for the shake of organization's security, freely future development may perceive risks of using the Open Source Software.

But some believe that the most reliable indication of the future of Open Source is its tremendous growth. They argued that in just a few years, Open Source Software movement has gone from nothing to a robust body of software that solves different problems and is reaching the million-user count. There is no reason for discarding it for implementation to different organizations including Library and Information Science organizations.

Bretthauer[8] notes that this is not a risk for using open source software and he also comments that vendors of proprietary software can "withdraw the product, discontinue its support, go out of business, and/or can be acquired by another vendor who can do any of the above". Members of Open Software community often set up mutual support mechanisms, sometimes based on an email discussion list. It is possible for another organisation to take on the role of project "co-ordinator", if the project originator is unable to continue the responsibility. This has happened with the MyLibrary project, with support shifting from North Carolina State University to Notre Dame University when the project's main developer, Eric Lease Morgan, changed jobs.

In conclusion, it can be argued that adopting Open Source Software for management of libraries and information centers are increasing in India and the World. The success factors for adopting open source software in library organization require the same type of evaluation as purchasing commercial software. Libraries, in India, may think of adopting Open

Source Software for their house keeping and other managerial applications.

References

1. The Keystone Principles: An action plan for values-based librarianship. *C&RL News.* 61(2) February 2000.
2. http://www.webopedia.com.
3. http://www.opensource.org.
4. International Encyclopedia of Information and Library Science. 2nd. ed. Ed. By John Feather and Paul Sturges. London: Routledge, 2003. p.468.
5. Reitz, Joan M. : Dictionary for Library and Information Science. London: Libraries Unlimited, 2005. p.503-504.
6. Deka, Dipen : The Role of open Source Software in Building Institutional Repository. *In* Manojkumar, K. : Proceedings Digital Preservation, Management and Access to Information in the Twenty First Century: 4th Convention PLANNER – 2006. p.121-127.
7. http://www.domainsmagazine.com/managearticle.asp [Chawner, Brenda: Free/Open Source Software: New Opportunities, New Challenges].
8. Bretthauer, David : Open source software in libraries. *Library Hi Tech News* 18 (5). 2001. p. 8-9.

Chapter 7

E-Publications as Helpful Resources for Researchers of Indian Libraries

"Study the past if you would refine the future" – said Confucius. This is the primary need for starting investigation or research. What is the meaning of research? The meaning of the research is stated in 'The Advanced Learner's Dictionary of Current English' thus: "a careful investigation or enquiry specially through search for new facts in any branch of knowledge".[1] Actually research is an academic activity, which has systematic technical processes of its own. The aim of research is to find out the truth which is hidden and has not yet been discovered, so is the voyage of discovery. Research has some processes or methods which may be as under :

(*a*) defining the research problem,

(*b*) redefining the existing problems,

(*c*) formulating hypothesis on the research problem,

(*d*) collecting facts or data,

(*e*) organizing facts or data,

(*f*) evaluating facts or data,

(*g*) reaching conclusions in the way of suggesting solutions,

(*h*) testing the conclusions to determine whether they fit the formulating hypothesis towards the concerned research problem, and finally,

(*i*) formulating theoretical or scientific principles towards the concerned research problem.

So, it is clear that research process has various steps. These steps do not necessarily follow each other in any specific order. However, the researcher should keep in mind the various steps of research processes, which will act as useful procedural guideline regarding his/her research in progress :

1. formulating the research problem;
2. extensive literature survey;
3. developing the hypothesis;
4. preparing the research designing;
5. determining the sample design;
6. collecting the data;
7. execution of the project;
8. analysis of data;
9. hypothesis testing;
10. generalizations and interpretation; and
11. preparation of the report or presentation of the results, *i.e.* formal write-up of conclusions reached.[2]

1. Traditional Library System and Research

Before 1980s it was the primary task of a researcher to issue letters to Research Institutes and University Departments about the on going research on the topic, related topics, allied topics, etc. They also issued letters to the librarians of those institutes on the same queries. Finally, after receiving answers the researcher or scientist used to visit different institutions or libraries to access his/her required literature or documents. Librarians of different national level institutes like INSDOC, NASSADOC, National Library, etc. received huge number of requests for making bibliographies on a particular topic chosen by the researchers. The same librarians also received queries on research progress in different subject areas from new entrants into research. Actually, these were very helpful information to the new researchers and with these they select their reading materials. According to the received information they wrote to the authors of the article for a reprint of the article or tried to search different libraries where the materials can be found physically. Thus it can be said that the researchers were very much dependent on capable librarians for starting their research work or the quick progress of the same.

2. Need for Redesign of Library System

Observing these difficulties of the researchers and way

of services offered by the then librarians of the traditional libraries Wilson[3] opines for redesigning of library system. He argued in favour of redesigning of library system thus: "Universities library were designed primarily for the acquisition and handing of physical artifacts, but the rapid growth of electronics resources has called that design into question. The nature of access to information has been transformed by the emergence of the Internet, which has changed the ground rules for the production of and access to scholarly communication."

3. New Library Environments

The library situation has been changed because of the influence of Information Technology (IT), which has replaced the old method of supplying data, information and knowledge to the researchers or society. The huge out-comings of e-publications, *viz.* e-journals, e-databases, e-books etc. have changed the earlier situation. These large numbers of e-publications have been brought out through the world, which are easily available in the publishers' website through browsing Internet. Libraries have adopted redesigning the organizational system with the application of IT equipments, by creating local area network and procuring required hardware and software. In this changed environment, almost all big libraries, librarians are helping their researchers or users to make connections only. Librarians may procure print items as their own resources for their institutional libraries vis-à-vis e-publications such as e-journals, e-databases, e-books,e-bibliographical databases, e-reference tool-kits, etc., which will be helpful for creating rich electronic environment in the library.

Now a day technological changes in the publishing have enhanced the power of searching of researchers as well as the mode of accesses of information. The technological changes have influenced the relationship and behavior models of researcher to a great deal which surprises the researcher to have results within few moments on his/her research queries thus:

- What has been published in my research areas?
- Who are the leading researchers in my field of research?

- Like print secondary source journals (abstracting, indexing journals) on-line abstract databases are searchable.
- Like the print originals digital back files are fully searchable which contain the complete text of journals from the first issue of the journals, *i.e.*, archives.
- Most relevant articles on research topic are also available through on-line citations.

4. E-Publishers and Indian Libraries

Some of the world famous publishers have taken initiative to help librarians for providing electronic environment. They have created state-of-the-art IP based searching and linking functionality, and navigated via a simple and intuitive user interface. Librarian may invest money for these e-documents as they are usually renew or subscribe print journals. Some times these e-facilities are available on the same cost, or 10% to 15% more investment. Here, the facilities have provided more than investment because, most of this type of e-access provide archives facilities for a specific period or from the very beginning of the journal, *i.e.* from volume one. If the library goes to consortium, then e-journals or databases would be available at a very low price. Some times there are packages which can be accepted as per the need and fund provision of the library. A good librarian has to match the need and fund always. It may be said that in the new electronic environment a librarian can be assessed as successful on the basis of the utilization of library fund, to cover the research areas in progress or to cover future possible research areas of his/her own research institute or university.

4.1 : E-publications Available for Indian Libraries

It is a known fact that recent technological developments have changed the library environment as the availability of information in e-format or machine readable format are increasing day by day. This is definitely a transition period and now libraries are gradually transforming into multimedia libraries, electronic libraries, digital libraries, etc. The emphasis now developed in libraries to procure e-documents either to store them in their storage server or to create link to the publishers' website directly. Here libraries are interested to take essential programmes so that readers should have the automated library environment for on-line information access and retrieval facilities as and when they required. This situational change of Indian libraries has been observed by different e-publishers and they are producing different types of e-publications suitable for providing library services in research libraries in India. These presently produced available e-documents are of various types :

(*a*) standards,

(*b*) patents,

(*c*) gateway portals,

(*d*) e-journal,

(*e*) e-databases,

(*f*) e-books,

(*g*) e-reference books, etc.

4.2 : Electronic Version of Indian Standards and Patents

Indian standard are now available in CD-ROM. Any library can subscribe the entire collection of Indian standards more than 19 thousand in numbers on annuals subscription basis there is a facilities for (bi-monthly) periodic updates during subscription period. It is permissible to copy of these copyrighted items for the internal use of researchers or for fair use. These standards can also be available on segment wise subscription basis that helps the special libraries collection building or the low budgeted technical libraries and their researchers.

Now Indian Patent Database available on Internet at http://www.indianpatents.org.in. Patent database can be available on CDROM. Each has been priced at Rs. 500/- (Five hundred only). Alternatively, under the membership scheme annual CDs shall be made available for both databases on a quarterly basis. The subscriber shall get four CDs each of the two databases updated every quarter. The scheme can be availed by sending the annual subscription fee of Rs. 3500/- (Three Thousand and five hundred only).

4.2.1 : Gateway Portals

There are some e-gateway portals available for Indian libraries. Some of these are very much beneficial for the library and its researchers that are extending huge retrieval facilities to millions of pages of published journals abstracts, full-text articles, reports, technical magazines, international news papers, news based and popular magazines, etc. IP based limited/unlimited retrieval facilities are available for gateway portals. Some examples of available gateway portals are to be shown in table-1.

Table 1 : Some Available E-gateways Portals for Indian Libraries

Name of Gateway Portals	*Subject Coverage*	*Websites*
E-gateway	Various Subjects	www.murugan.in
J-Gate	Various Subjects	www.j-co.ingate.informindia.
JCC@Indest	Science and Engineering	www.jcc-indest.informindia.co.in/about/about.asp
OpenMED@NIC	Medical and allied Sciences	http://openmed.nic.in/
SciGate	Science, Engineering, Medical & Management	http://www.ncsi.iisc.ernet.in/scigate-about.php/

4.2.2 : E-Journal Websites

The following are the well known world famous high standard e-journal websites on different subjects are available for Indian libraries. Some of the subjects are : Civil Engineering, Mechanical Engineering, Computer Engineering Sciences, Physics, Chemistry, Life Sciences, Literature, Humanities and Social Sciences, etc. These websites cover items full-text articles from journals, magazines, periodicals, conference proceedings, transactions, bibliographical records abstracts, and reference works with citation links. Some examples of available full-text e-resources for Indian libraries are to be shown in table-2.

4.2.3 : E-Databases (Bibliographical)

The mostly used e-databases in Indian libraries are on abstracts and indexing of resources, which provides clue to new researcher for further studies. The available e-databases are on the subjects: Civil, Mechanical, Electrical and Electronic Engineering; Computer Science; Information Technology; Physics; Chemistry; Mathematics; Agriculture; Applied Life Sciences; Microbiology; Plant Sciences, etc. Some of these special type e-resources for Indian libraries are mentioned in Table 3.

4.2.4 : E-Books and E-Reference Books

Some leading publishers like Taylor and Francis, Routledge, Psychology Press, CRC Press, Oxford University Press, Sage Publications, etc. have now devoted to publish e-books. Presently, e-books have become more and more popularized in world class libraries. Librarians of Indian libraries are also showing great interest for e-books and e-reference books. Some of these available e-resources are noted in Table 4.

5. Consortiums Available in India

To share valuable scholarly e-publications or e-contents depicting new inventions, discoveries, innovative measures and state-of-arts of different domains of science consortium have been established in India. It is true that price of the science journals are very high. Again it is also true that some basic journals are to be required to subscribe in different scientific institutions for conducting research. To avoid subscribing multiple print copies of same journals it has been planned to subscribe huge number of e-journals for each of the research institutions under the consortium. Some of the science consortiums are available for Indian Libraries are to be found in Table 5.

6. Librarians and E-publications

On promotion of e-journals, e-books, e-databases, e-portals the publishers have designed their products in such a way that these products will help the librarian thus :

- IP based access for full-text journals, books, databases through web site.
- Help desk support for the librarian.
- Comprehensive user support materials.
- Periodical usage reports.
- Registering users interest through mail-box.
- Regular information update to the user through e-mail.
- Complementary mimeographed print issues, where possible.

7. Conclusions

University or Research libraries or Academic libraries are now in the digital age, so it is necessary to reshape or re-design these libraries in such a way that they will be able to improve the services they provide to the teachers, scholars and students both for the present and the future. As a result of rapid environmental changes, interference of information technology, libraries or academic libraries mainly of university libraries are needed to think reorganize the present the present structure, which is an attempt to meet changing information need and expectation of users to provide greater effectiveness and efficient manner.

If the research institutes transit towards e-collection development for their libraries it will certainly provide some good impacts in respect enrichment of journal collections and services to the readers or researchers.[4] The key impacts on libraries include the following :

(*a*) Libraries can own copies of journals or articles from OA or OA journals.

(*b*) Libraries accure rights to archive with no special permission from publishers or periodic payments.

(*c*) Access to and usages of OA resources are not limited.

(*d*) No question of infringement of law or violation of copyrights.

(*e*) Free from hassles of discontinuation or gaps for receiving journals or articles.

Table 2 : Some Available Full-Text E-resources for Indian Libraries

Full Text E-Resources	*Items Covered With Subjects*	*Website*
ACM Digital Library	Journals, Magazines, Conference Proceedings and Bibliographical Records on Computer Science.	http://portal.acm.org/dl.cfm
ASCE Journals	Journals, Periodicals and Transactions in civil engineering.	www.pubs.asce.org/journals/
ASME Journals	Journals and Transactions in mechanical engineering.	http://www.asme.org/Publications/Journals/View_Journals_Online.cfm
Science Direct	Journals, Magazines, Citation Links Bibliographical databases, Abstracts, Conference Proceedings, Reference. Works on, Physics, Computer Sciences, Engineering, etc.	www.sciencedirect.com
Springer Link	Journals, books on Science, Engineering, Humanities	http://springerlink.com
Sage Full-text Collections	Journals, Back Files, Reference Works or Citation Links.	www.sagepublications.com
Project MUSE	Different Subjects mainly Literature, Humanities and Social Sciences.	http://muse.jhu.edu/journals/

Table 3 : Some Available E-Databases (Bibliographical) for Indian Libraries

Name of the Databases	*Subjects and Coverage*	*Website*
INSPEC on EI Village	Bibliographic database on physics, electronic engineering, Computer Sc., Inf. technology, etc.	http://www.tau.ac.il/scilib/Elvillage.html
COMPENDEX on EI Village	Abstracts of Journal Articles, Conference proceedings, Reports, etc. on Engineering.	www.ovid.com/site/catalog/DataBase/53.jsp?
MathSciNet	AMS database of more than a million reviews and abstracts of math publications.	www.ams.org/mathscinet/ -
SciFinder Scholar	CAS Database including Chemical Abstract.	www.cas.org/products/sfacad/index.html
CAB Abstracts	Database of over 5 Million records covering Plant Sciences, Agriculture, Applied life Sciences, Microbiology.	http://www.cabi.org/datapage.asp?iDocID=165

Table 4 : Some of the Available E-Books and E-Reference Books Resources for Indian Libraries

Name of the E-Books and E-Reference Books Resources	*Subjects and Coverage*	*Website*
Sage e-Reference	On-line 47 encyclopedias on different subjects	www.sage-ereference.com/public/home.php
Taylor & Francis eBooks	On-line 16000 eBooks and Reference Works	www.informaworld.com
Britanica	Encyclopedia Britanica	www.eb.com.
Oxford eReference	American National Biography Online	http://www.oup.com/online/#anb

Table 5 : Some Available Consortium for Indian Libraries

Name of the Consortium	*Subjects and Coverage*	*Website*
Forum for Resource Sharing in Astronomy and Astrophysics (FORSA)	Astronomy & Astrophysics	http://www.iiap.res.in/library/forsa.html
Virtual Information Centre (VIC)	E-Journals	http://www.vic-ikp.info/
National Institute of Science Communication & Information Resources (NISCAIRE)	Provides access to 4000+ journals plus 2000 Licensed & Open access Science, Technology & Medical journals	http://www.niscair.res.in/
Indian National Digital Library in Engineering Science and Technology (INDEST-AICTE)	E-resources in Science, Technology & Engineering Information to IITs, NITs, IIM, etc.	http://indest.iitd.ac.in
Information Network (UGC-INFONET)	Provides access to 7000+ journals and databases to Universities.	http://www.inflibnet.earnet.in
Health Information Network (HELINET)	Provides access to Health Science Information.	http://ijgate-helinet.informindia.co.in
Indira Gandhi Centre for Atomic Research (IGCAR)	Provides access to 1700 journals and back files on Physics, Computer Sc. and Engineering Information to Atomic Research Institutes	http://www.igcar.ernet.in/

Now, the library can make provision for a laboratory where at least 10 PCs have to be reserved for the researchers and then it will be possible to browse on-line library resources: library catalogues, full text research journals, bibliographic databases, thesis databases, patents, standards, CD-ROMs, e-books and other reference works. Libraries may provide searching or browsing facilities to the researchers' free or a nominal charge be fixed for downloading full-text articles, which generates fund and that can also be utilized for the promotion of better services and adding costly collections for their libraries.

References

1. The Advanced Learner's Dictionary of Current English. Oxford: Oxford University Press, 1952. p.1069.
2. Kothari, C.R.: Research methodology: methods and techniques. New Delhi: Wishwa Prakashan, 2003.
3. Wilson, T.D.: Redesigning the university library in the digital age. *Journal of Documentation.* 54 (1), 1998. p.15-27. [As stated Moran, Barbara B.: Restructuring the university library: a North American perspective. *Journal of Documentation.* 57 (1), 2001. p.100-114].
4. Mondal, M. and Panda, K.C.: Global access to science information: the changing dynamics of access and practices in India. The paper presented in the Conference Program on Global Access to Science Scientific Publishing for the future: IATUL 2007 held on June 11-14, 2007 at Stockholm, Sweden.

Chapter 8

Developing Skills of Library Professionals for Using Information and Communication Technology (ICT)

The term Information and Communication Technology (ICT) was used as synonymous with Information Technology, since few years back. Now a day, due to vast advancement of communication technologies and particularly the INTERNET, the term is more popular as ICT. Peter Wright describes this situation in the way: "As educators worked at explore the potentials of microcomputer, a quite revolution was underway in the world of telecommunications, and thus suddenly (seemingly) there was Internet"[1]. It refers to a broad spectrum of techniques to help its users to get, produce, and share ideas and resources. It is used as a tool for 'leapfrogging' stages of development.

In fact, ICT is a tool developed with the help of a set of technologies. According to Peter Wright, it can be said, "terms and technologies that fall under the umbrella of ICT include calculator, applications, tools, computer assisted instruction (CAI), the WWW, alternative delivery, and on-line learning"[2]. The definition of ICT has cited in the website-www.ictadvice.org.uk thus: "Information and communications technologies (ICT) are the computing and communications facilities and features that variously support teaching, learning and a range of activities in education"[3].

ICT is used for information process and management and it is not restricted to a particular discipline. The application of ICT has spread its roots in different areas of knowledge. The use of ICT has increased in the field of engineering, education, medical science, economics, business, management, Library and Information Science, etc.

1. ICT in Library and Information Science

The term ICT is extensively used in Library and Information Centres and Library and Information Science Education (LISE). ICT acts as tool for information management and use in Library and Information Centres. According to Rashid Hussain, ICT is used "Not only to code and process data, but also to manage information and processes to achieve more efficient and effective results by optimizing the management of resources, the flow of information and know-how"[4].

2. Librarians and ICT

The working librarians should have the proper knowledge of ICT, if not acquired it beforehand to enter in the library profession. It is very much required because, the library environment has dramatically changed with the influence of ICT, which has recently accepted and accommodated in the field of Library and Information Science and library services. The library clienteles are becoming more sophisticated in placing their demand to the librarian for information. So, the librarian should have the basic concept and skill of ICT to handle the changed situation.

Now most of the library professionals have the preliminary idea of ICT and they aware that the main component of ICT is Internet, which can be used to facilitate the library and its professionals in the following way :

(*a*) To access other sites and sources of expertise relating to one's query or search.

(*b*) To share of resources with other libraries.

(*c*) To collaborate different library projects or developmental issues.

(*d*) To make communications (e-mail, videoconferencing, etc.).

(*e*) To search collaborating library databases for introducing improved system of acquisition, cataloguing, and reference services in parent library; etc.

(*f*) To develop professional activities.

3. Need for Training of Library Professionals in ICT

The term training means an attempt to improve the skill level of worker or professionals. The training may be of two kinds, formal and informal, which creating awareness, new knowledge and building confidence in the mind of workers. It requires for the following purposes :

1. Developing competitive approach.
2. Increasing individual skills, concept and understanding of the daily jobs.
3. Understanding the area of new working environment.
4. Realizing the goal and objective of the organization, and expectation of organization.
5. Identifying the alternatives work procedure in environmental change.
6. Providing current information regarding development and job situation.
7. Building a new team or personnel group.
8. Gaining knowledge and skills for managing the organization in new environment.
9. Creating further opportunity for training.

In case of library organization for introduction of ICT the training is most essential for improvement of skills of library professionals and it is a continuous process in library like other organizations.

It is true that most of the senior library professionals in India have little practical or real knowledge on ICT, because the ICT has been introduced in Library and Information curriculum very recently. Young generation librarians may possess even good account of knowledge of operating and procedure of ICT. Majority of librarians should acquire knowledge of ICT on account of changed environment of the libraries, the increased automation and digitization of information acquisition, processing, storage and retrieval pattern. It is also true that library professionals have to constantly update their knowledge and skill for providing ICT based information services as per the demand of readers. And therefore, the necessary provision for proper training programme on ICT is required which could extend the basic knowledge and skill of library professionals.

Actually, there are four general skill categories basic literacy, technical, interpersonal and problem solving, which can be achieved through training. Training can include every thing, from teaching employees basic reading skills to advance courses in executive leadership.

3.1. Major Training areas on ICT for Library Professionals

The followings have been identified as major areas or aspects on ICT for Librarians :

- Handling CD Rom databases and work station.
- Managing Multimedia library.
- Browsing Internet.
- Operation of Library Management Software.
- Web designing and web hosting.
- Managing on-line full text journals.
- Providing on-line reference service.
- Bar coding and Inventory management system.
- Media centers.
- Video conferencing.
- E-journal management.
- E-publishing and e-learning.
- Digitizing of old and rare library documents.
- Data mining and warehousing.
- Installing and managing library servers.
- Networking systems.
- Security systems.

4. Training Methods

Training methods may be classified as : (*a*) formal and (*b*) informal[5]. In case of formal training organization plans in advance and that has a structured format and it is a lengthy process. Again, informal training has no formal structure. It is unplanned and may be taken/adopted within a very short period or notice. The concern organization management adopts it as and when necessity arises for the organization, its situation changes and individual or personel needs for learning skills, and for keeping employees' update or current.

Actually, any library can arrange formal training of its own and within the library organization itself. Suppose, in case of Visva-Bharati Library, the Librarian has decided to switch over traditional library housekeeping system into automated process by introducing IT. The Librarian may convince the Visva-Bharati Library Committee and the Vice-Chancellor for the creation of this new library environment and finally, the appropriate authority has sanctioned the money. Then with the help of suitable IT consultant and vendor the new library environment has been created in a particular time frame. Thus, LAN has been set up with FOC throughout the university campus. Total cable length is nearly 15 kilometers. After that, the Librarian Visva-Bharati Library has to select the best 'library management software' and to organize on site training for its library professionals who can handle easily the software for library operation. This is an example of planned training programme and this is to be called formal training.

In reality, informal training arranges by the employees themselves. When working in real situation in Visva-Bharati Library IT environment (by handling library software LIBSYS-4 Unicode) professional 'X', who is an employee of the same library, may ask his/her fellow colleague 'Y' for tips for the completion of a specific item of job or the whole process. Thus the professional 'X' learns from professional 'Y', which is an example informal training in library organization.

Training methods may also be classified as: on the job training and off the job training. On the job training in library means to train employees to improve skills through library's own working environment. It includes job rotation, apprenticeship, and new assignment under the guidance or supervision of a senior professional. Off the job training in library means to train library professionals for improving their skills outside the library organization. It includes classroom lectures, seminars, group activities, Internet courses, satellite-beamed video-tapes/lecture materials, video-conferences, self study programmes, etc. To improve skills of the library professionals, libraries should have to implement this training programme.

4.1 : Formal Training Methods

In case of formal training of library professionals the following methods may be adopted :

- Participatory lectures.
- Practical demonstrations.
- Field activities.
- Learning by experience through visits.
- Hand on experience.

4.2 : Training Resources

There are some training resources, which may be applied to train the library professionals as under :

- Reading of key journals.
- Brochure of new technological products or equipment or software of manufacturers.
- Demonstration for the new technological products or equipment or software of manufacturers.
- Professional or subject experts.
- Professional bodies.
- Government agencies.
- Attending Seminar and Conferences.
- Participating Workshops and Training Courses.

4.3 : Training Multiplier Effect Method

Training multiplier effect actually applies in large-scale industry or high technological sector. In a country where the new industry or technology is being introduced first time and the country lacks the high standard or quality technological background, then only Training Multiplier Effect method is applied[6]. It means foreign lending of some skilled people for a specific period to a nation for their local people in a particular industry to learn the technical know-how for introducing advance technology. During this period, those foreign technologists or specialists train some local people and they gained the technological know-how properly which make them national or local specialist or skilled personnel. Thus the foreign know-how came to nation. Now these local skilled people or group would be the local trainer and they finally train the entire unskilled local personnel of that particular industry or high technology sector. This Training Multiplier Effect method can be applied to the field of library organization for introducing ICT for library operation and application tool.

4.4 : Application of Training Multiplier Effect Method in Libraries

In a particular library, where most operation and services are going on traditional way, the background of those library professionals would naturally be largely traditional. If the authority of the library needs to introduce automated environment in the same library, the majority library professionals would urgently require training within very short period. For improving working situation of the library, it may be true that in the local library culture or environment is not familiar with advance technological improvement by introduction of ICT in library field. And in that case "Training Multiplier Effect" model will be much effective, which has shown as the Training Multiplier Effect (TME) model for the library in Figure 1.

4.5 : Senior Librarian and TME

For the implementation of TME model in any library organization a team should be constituted along with Senior Librarians. The formation of the team may vary library to library according to the nature, size, staff strength, and out look of the authority. But the Senior Librarians Team must include some key strategies and managerial responsibilities Among other strategic responsibilities, the senior management team should have general responsibility in relation to ICT. These responsibilities can be categorized under five broad headings as :

(*a*) Strategic direction and development of the library.

(*b*) Teaching and learning.

(*c*) Leading and managing staff.

(*d*) Efficient and effective deployment of staff and resources, and

(*e*) Accountability.

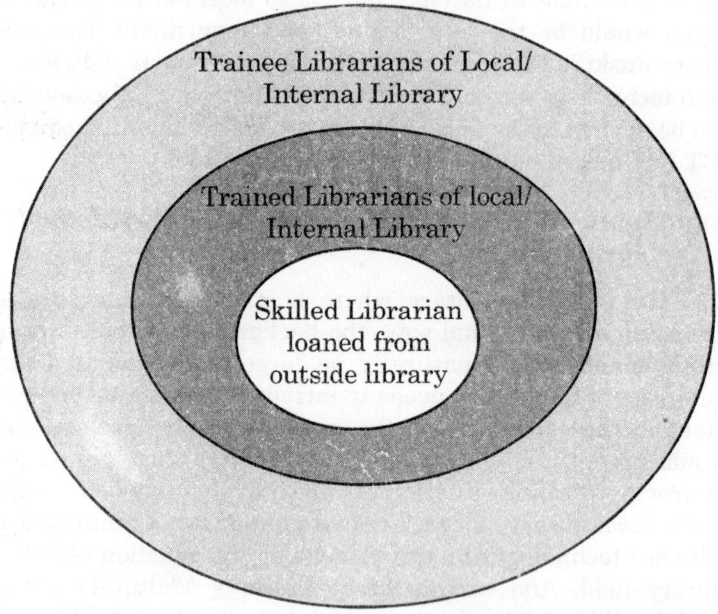

Fig. 1 : Training Multiplier Effect Model for libraries where majority of library professionals need training for using of ICT.

5. Conclusion

Each and every Library should have the human development planning because most libraries have taken drives to enter into changed environment and turned in right direction to perform different task areas of the Library using IT. To cater better library services to the end users, man power planning would be very helpful as it improves the skill of the librarian and library professional of the particular library.

How we can have skilled librarian or library professionals for the present changed scenario for introducing and maintenance of ICT activities or services?

- By creation of some technical posts and new recruitment.
- To fill up the existing vacant technical posts, and
- To introduce training for the existing technical staffs or professionals.

It would be easy to have good and sound Information Technology knowledgeable librarians or professionals for the Library as the Library and Information Science schools or departments have updated their course curriculum or syllabus according to new requirement for the modern library and information centers. But creation of new posts and new recruitments not depend on the Library Management Body, it depends on the higher authority or funding authority. Moreover, the creation of new post and to fill up that and filling up the existing vacant post are lengthy process.

So, the Library should opt for the third concept i.e. to introduce training for the existing technical staffs or professionals. It is true that the majority of library professionals, who are most competent in course of recruitment and present continuing set up of working system of the library. It is also true that competent employee do not remain competent forever during the working life. Skills of existing employee of any library deteriorate and may become absolute in changed environment. So it is necessary for each and every library management body to make proper arrangement so that the majority of the library professionals improve their skill and competency by way of training method.

References

1. Wright, Peter (ed.) : Information and Communication Technology and the Mathematics Classroom. *In* Encyclopedia of Library Science, Vol. 71. New York: Marcel Dekkar, 2000. p. 189-208
2. *Ibid.*
3. http://www.ictadvicc.org.uk.
4. Hussain, Rashid: Role of Information Communication Technology in Rural Development. *In* Information Support for Rural Development : XXI National Seminar of IASLIC, Jadavpur University, Kolkata. p. 143-148.

5. Robbins, Stephen P. : Organizational behavior. 9th ed. New Delhi: Prentice Hall, 2001.
6. Newstrom, J.W. and Davis, K. : Organisational behaviour at work. 4th. Ed. New Delhi: Tata McGraw Hill., 2002. p. 396-397.

Chapter 9

Application of Knowledge Management in Library and Information Centre

Libraries have been performing the most vital role as storehouses of human thoughts, aspirations, wisdom, wits, knowledge and art, since the dawn of civilization. The written records in any form, in sign or alphabet; in any media, made of clay, papyrus, parchment or paper and which kept alive the human knowledge has been preserved by libraries generation after generation. With the help of these human records the present human society has became increased and developed so. Again, in society human knowledge increased at a very high rate and thus Science, Philosophy, Literature, Arts, Social Sciences, etc. has been exploring new frontiers day by day.

Now, the society has become more and more complex. The developments of societies depend on the communication of new knowledge to its people and thus society demands for good communication system. Accordingly, the communication means become more and more complex: primitive sounds and signs give way to highly developed spoken and written languages; invention; and technical skill produce varied media-printed books, telecommunications, films, sound recordings, computers, information technology, etc. From generations past it was the need for humankind that ever-increasing amount of new information and knowledge must flow smoothly and accurately, not only between the members of the same society but also between one to another society.

Actually, knowledge becomes more valuable to the humankind. All that we do, all that we make, all that we earn are to be treated as knowledge. This knowledge is always altered by new knowledge and also by technological developments. Thus, there is a growing need to become easier with use of knowledge and for the same it is necessary to manage the knowledge effectively so that it can be used with its full benefit. Hence, we see the rise of Knowledge Management [KM], which has came out as one of the important sub-category of General Management. The term 'knowledge management' [KM] has been used in many subject fields for years long. The term KM is recently discussed in the field of Library and Information Science.

1. Definition

The definition of 'knowledge management' [KM] is confusing as there are many definitions of the term. Some of the definitions are cited here with some interpretations.

The simplest definition given by Davanport[1] as: "knowledge management is the process of capturing, distributing, and effectively using the knowledge". This definition indicates KM has three systematic steps: knowledge capturing, its distribution and effective use.

According to Duhon[2], KM is : "A discipline that promotes an integrated approach to identifying, capturing, evaluating, retrieving, and sharing all of an enterprises information assets. These assets may include databases, documents, policies, procedures and previously un-captured expertise and experience in individual workers". This definition clarifies that KM includes conventional information and knowledge units of an organization as well as 'tacit knowledge', which means the knowledge, which is known but not yet captured in any formal or explicit way or fashion.

Another definition given by Ruggles[3] thus : "Knowledge management is a newly emerging, interdisciplinary business model dealing with all aspects of knowledge within the context of the firm, including knowledge creation, codification, sharing, learning and innovation. Some aspects of this process are facilitated with information technologies, but knowledge management is to a greater degree, about organisational culture and practices". One very important dimension to KM has been emphasized here i.e. culture of the organization, in this definition.

A comprehensive definition given by DeLong and Seemann[4] may be stated as "The development of tools, processes, systems structures and cultures explicitly to improve the creation, sharing, and use of knowledge critical for decision making".

As a formal definition from American Productivity Center[5,6] : 'Knowledge Management is a conscious strategy of getting the right knowledge to the right people at the right time and helping people share and put information into action in ways that strive to improve organizational performance'. This definition is very similar to S.R. Ranganathan definition for Library Reference Service.

Actually, the exact meaning of the term KM depends on the users. It is found that two general trends have been emerged to represent the term KM in case of literature and actual practice. Luthans[7] has noted this and he grouped the KM into two as: tangible knowledge, and intangible knowledge. According to him, organization structures and systems, *e.g.*, R&D (research and development) outcomes, patents, copyrights, royalties, licenses, and information on employees, customers, suppliers, products and competitors are the issues of tangible knowledge; and the intelligence, experience, skill and ideas as possessed by employees and other stakeholders (customers, suppliers, owners, consultants, etc.) associated with the organization are the issues of intangible knowledge.

KM is to be regarded as bringing tacit knowledge to the surface, consolidating it in forms by which it would be widely accessible, and promoting its continuing creation. KM is an added dimension emphasizing the need for the integration of explicit and tacit knowledge. It is the holistic management of information, people and processes with an enabler.

KM is a set of processes of elicitation, transformation, and diffusion of intellectual capital primarily residing as tacit knowledge in individuals that led to innovation, knowledge creation, and replenishment of the organizations core competency throughout an enterprise so that it can be shared and thus reused. It helps organizations to find, select, organize, disseminate, and transfer important information. It also helps to provide expertise necessary for activities such as problem solving, dynamic learning, strategic planning, and decision-making.

2. The Normal Task of Knowledge Managers

The tasks of Knowledge Manager includes the identification of knowledge (explicit and tacit) needs and assess the design, development and implementation of KM strategies and solutions in order to satisfy the needs of the organization[8]. Identifying the tasks of Knowledge Manager, Snowden[9] points out that all of us have to win the hearts and minds of individuals at all levels. Streatfield and Wilson[10] feel that all key staffs should be treated as Knowledge Managers, even if one of them assumes overall responsibility for the strategy. Normally, Librarian has to do with the records of human knowledge, which needs to organize, develop, store, disseminate and so on the basis of this nature of job, he/she is to be accepted as the Knowledge Manager.

3. Information Technology and KM

The Information Technology [IT] has a great role over the KM. Library acquires and store information with the help of IT. Treating knowledge as tangible asset, KM employs IT to acquire and store information as products of the library or the organization and make delivery to its users or customers. For this purpose some specific KM programmes need to be taken as under :

(*a*) Establishing of repository databases and retrieval system.

(*b*) Gathering information from customers.

(*c*) Creating and maintaining employee talent and skill profiles, and

(*d*) Creating and maintaining virtual or physical platforms for sharing and disseminating information.[11]

McCune[12] has argued that some technology backups are essentially needed for the application of KM, which can be shown as :

3.1 : Connectivity

1. Computer networks, including LAN, WAN, or Internet access.
2. E-mail.

3.2 : Storage

1. Data warehouse, data marts, and assorted databases.
2. Document and management programme.
3. Electronic directories of "experts," such as corporate Yellow Pages and expert systems that compile information from experts in an intelligent database.
4. Large storage capacities, usually a corporate Internet.

3.3 : Locators

1. Browsers, which search through corporate Internets.
2. Agents, software that seeks out information.
3. "Knowledge maps," indicates that classify information and help users determine the location of the information.
4. Metadata or electronic card catalogues, summerise and categorise data.
5. "Push" technology, which lets users request that all information on a particular topic be forwarded to them.

3.4 : Learning Vehicles

1. Distance learning applications that help employees to acquire knowledge.

3.5 : Recent Developments

2. "Knowledge portals" available on employees' individual desktop PCs or PDAs for easy access to all useful data in the organization.
3. Software that transforms text and numbers into charts and graphs to make it easier to glean relevant information.
4. More sophisticated filters, browsers, and locators to make it possible for users to make queries and receive answers in regular language.

A good KM system is always acts as ever growing dynamic system. Knowledge is a resource and it is not consumed when used, it can be used again and again as and when required, over the ages or time, even in the changed environment. As knowledge is disseminated, individuals may develop it, identify a new knowledge and finally return to the system. And, thus, the knowledge repository grows over time. This is very similar with the Ranganathan's 'Fifth Law of Library Science'.

4. KM versus Library and Information Management

Some of the library and information scientists often expressed their views that KM is just the new name for 'information resource management' and this again was a new name for 'documentation in librarianship'. But it is true that there are some real differences in emphasis between KM and traditional library and information work. These key differences have been identified by Koeing[13] and laid down here with some modifications in table 1.

Table 1 : Key Differences in Emphasis Between KM and Traditional Library and Information Work

Knowledge Management (KM)	*Traditional Library and Information Work*
1	*2*
1. Emphasis upon unstructured and informal information/ knowledge.	1. Emphasis upon structured and formal information/knowledge with some limitation.
2. Emphasis on internal information and external information, which resides with supplier and customer, not in the open literature.	2. Emphasis on information, external to the organisation, 'the literature'.
3. Active role in corporate culture, transformation and change agentry.	3. Neutrality within the organisation.
4. Information and knowledge sharing, in context of a dense web structure.	4. Information and knowledge delivery, as a hub (library) and spoke structure.

(Contd...)

1	2
5. A loose unformed poorly developed appreciation for information and knowledge structuring.	5. Syntactic structures, information structuring, taxonomies, cataloging, classification.
6. Knowledge of the context, organisation, sectoral (industry) supplier, customer.	6. Growing contextual knowledge, but not well recognised within the organisation.
7. An aware of knowledge as text, but coming from a background in non-textual information.	7. Information primarily as text, secondarily as numerical or graphic.
8. Linking knowledge sharing with compensation policy.	8. Has never been involved with compensation policy.

5. Need for KM in Libraries

Libraries from the very inception have been played the pivotal role to act as storehouses of knowledge and key enablers to spread learning in the society and its development. In all libraries librarians generally cater three services to their clientele :

(*a*) Reference Service,

(*b*) Reading Room Service, and

(*c*) Circulation Service for long years back manually/by hand operation.

These pivotal roles of libraries and librarians have been dramatically changed during 1990's onwards, because of tremendous development of IT and its attachment to libraries. For the IT development, a new dimension, a new environment is now taken place in the field of library services for the augmentation of library automation. The library environment has now basically changed the approaches of library users, their information requirements. The librarian today is expected to access, assess and classify the knowledge being generated throughout the world and integrate it with the information available in the particular library. To manage the users requirements, various information needs and all the approaches to information library system should be so organized that it would be able to meet the new challenges. The basic role of the Librarians/Information Professionals remains the same in the new environment as previous. The Library organizations/ Information Centers still expect that the Librarians/Information Professionals to acquire and organize information, make it available for use, disseminate it and, ultimately, dispose of information sources in all media and formats.

Thus, the role of librarians extends beyond the conventional librarianship. They need to have the understanding of subjects beyond superficial level. They must have know-how Internet technologies, which help in disseminating the information within an organization and provide accessibility to all pertinent library and other organizations to render services for its clientele crossing geographical location. This role of librarian is to be fruitful as and when library organisation accepts KM system for his/her own library. Only for this reason library organizations adopted KM into their field since late 1990's.

6. KM for University Libraries

KM should be applied to university libraries with the aim to enhance and improve the traditional library operations, to install a culture of sharing knowledge and to achieve the primary goals of the university library, to satisfy the library clientele by serving his requirement. KM will help to acquire the following deserved outcomes of the university library :

1. To enhance satisfaction of the library clientele.
2. To attract new library clientele.
3. To increase public faith through out the university organization.
4. To strive to meet and manage the rising expectations of library clientele.
5. To be able to justify the spending of allotted funds for library by the university.

The university library has to perform so many day-to-day activities to run the library smoothly. In the university library, those library activities are well categorized under different job areas and specific designated professionals are engaged for the jobs/tasks. As large number of library activities and services offered to the end users or clientele there is an immense possibility to adopt KM programme structures in university libraries for its managerial betterment. The following KM cycle may be accepted for the university library, which may be sketched in figure 1.

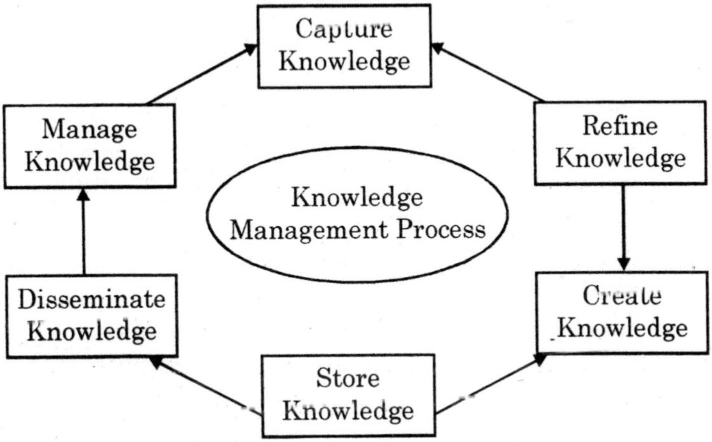

Figure 1 : Knowledge Management Cycle in a Library

The KM process of university library should have the above six stages or steps to be followed one after another. KM process of a library needs to follow this cyclic order. As knowledge is forever and it is always usable and reusable at any time by any end user of library organization. The above steps of the Knowledge Management process of the university library be explained thus :

1. ***Capture Knowledge*** : New knowledge must be identified as valuable and be represented in a reasonable way.
2. ***Refine Knowledge*** : New knowledge must be placed in context so that it is actionable.
3. ***Create Knowledge*** : Knowledge is created as people determine new ways of doing things or develop know how. Sometimes external knowledge is brought in.
4. ***Store Knowledge*** : Useful knowledge must then be stored in a reasonable format in a knowledge repository (library) so that others in the organization can access it.

5. ***Disseminate Knowledge*** : Knowledge must be made available in a useful format to anyone in the organization who needs it anywhere and anytime.
6. ***Manage Knowledge*** : In a library knowledge must be kept current. It must be reviewed to verify that it is relevant and accurate.

For the implementation of KM in any university library the followings are essential :

- By recruiting the best people for the library jobs.
- By exposing library professionals to the complexity of real problems to stimulate and cultivate professional know-how technologies.
- To retain library professionals to react fast in problem-solving techniques.
- To boost library professionals' problem solving abilities by capturing knowledge in systems and software.
- To overcome library professionals' reluctance for sharing information.

7. Conclusion

It is not easy to implement KM process to any organization. There are some barriers for the implementation of KM process. Turban and Aronson[14], O'Dell and Grayson[15] and Vass[16] have identified those barriers for the implementation of KM processes thus :

1. Ignorance - not knowing who has the right information required for the job; ignorance about the KM benefits.
2. Lack of time to find out and absorb the best participation recommended; and time lag taken to implement best practices recommended across departments.
3. Lack of relationship between the source and recipient of knowledge - absence of personal tie, credible and strong enough to justify listening and helping one another, *i.e.* culture does not encourage knowledge sharing.
4. No skill in KM techniques.
5. No commitment from senior manager on KM.

6. No funding for KM; Lack of appropriate technology for KM.

All the above barriers are common to any organization and are also true in case of university library organizations, which may be uprooted by active participation and tactful management of the librarian of the respective University.

It is true that university litrary readers are very much interested for searching webs for their purposes, e.g. higher education in India and abroad, research in progress, research opportunities in India and abroad, browsing abstracts and full-text journal articles, participation in Conference, Seminars, Workshops, etc. around the world and other relevant topics. The implication of Knowledge Management process in university libraries have already been taken to create a new culture among the library personnel and the clientele with the help of IT and KM System.

References

1. Davanport, T.H. : Coming soon: the CKO. *Information Week* 1994. p. 95.
2. Duhon, B. : It's all in our heads. *Inform.* 12(8), 1998. p. 9-13.
3. Ruggles, R : The state of the nation: knowledge management in practice. *California Management Review.* 40(Spring). 1998 p. 80-89.
4. DeLong, David and Seemann, Patrica : Confronting Conceptual Confusion and Conflict in Knowledge Management. *Organizational Dynamics,* 29(1). 2000. [As stated by Luthans, Fred : Organizational behavior. 9th. Ed. New York: McGraw-Hill, 2002.].
5. Teng, Sharon and Hawamdeh, Suliman : Knowledge management in public libraries. *Aslib Proceedings.* 54(3) 2002. p.188-197
6. American Productive Center : What is knowledge management? Available at : www.itconsultancy.com/extern/apqc.html [as stated by Teng, Sharon and Hawamdeh, Suliman: Knowledge management in public libraries. *Aslib Proceedings.* 54(3), 2002. p. 188-197.]
7. Luthans, Fred : Organizational behavior. 9th Ed. New York: McGraw-Hill 2002.

8. Synman, Retha M.M. : Do employers really know what they want? An analysis of the job advertisements for information and knowledge managers. *Aslib Proceedings.* 53(7), July-August 2001. p. 273-281.
9. Snowden, D. : A framework for creating a sustainable programme. *In* Knowledgement management: a real business guide. London : Caspian, 1998. p. 6-18.
10. Streatfield, D. and Wilson, T. : Deconstructing 'Knowledge management'. *Aslib Proceedings.* 51(3), 1999. p. 67-71.
11. Luthans, Fred. op. cit. p. 44.
12. McCune, C. : Thrust for the Knowledge. *Management Review.* April, 1999 p.12. [As stated by Luthans, Fred : Organizational behavior. 9th. Ed. New York: McGraw-Hill, 2002. p.44].
13. Koenig, Michael R. : Knowledge management. *In* Feather, John and Sturges, Paul (eds.) : International Encyclopedia of Information and Library Science. 2nd.ed. London: Routledge, 2003. p. 351-359.
14. Turban, E. and Aronson, J. : Decision Support System and intelligent systems. Delhi: Addision Wesley, 2001.
15. O'Dell, C. and Garyson, C.J. : If only we knew what we know. New York Free Press, 1998. [as stated by Teng, Sharon and Hawamdeh, Suliman: Knowledge management in public libraries. *Aslib Proceedings.* 54(3), 2002. p.188-197.].
16. Vass, L. : Brainstorming. *P C Week,* 16(22) 1999. [As stated by Turban, E. and Aronson, J.: Decision Support System and intelligentsystems. Delhi: Addision Wesley, 2001. p. 357].

Chapter 10

Copyright, Library and Library Services

Copyright is a right which prevents copying of an original work. It provides legal protection by the laws of any country to the authors of 'original works of authorship'. Copyright, as we mean today, has a historical process of development of at least 500 years as recorded information available.

Copyright may be defined as per Oxford English Dictionary as "The exclusive right given by law for a certain term of years to an author, composer, designer, etc. (or his assignee), to print, publish, and sell copies of his original work". The term is defined by the copyright act 1911 as "The sole right to produce or reproduce a work in any material from what so ever, to perform, or incase of a lecture, to deliver the work or any substantial part thereof in public; if work is unpublished to publish the work or any substantial part thereof".

1. Copyright: Historical Background

Copyright law has been existed in England since mid 16th century as Licensing Act. The law has been designed by the Crown in 1557 to maintain the govt. control over the press and monopolistic position of the stationers' company. This might best be defined as "stationer's copy right" "or publishers copyright" not the right of the authors as it is understood today. To control over the stationers or press at least two acts have been existed since long past which are known as :

(*a*) Legal Deposit and

(*b*) Delivery of Books Act.

The British copyright act of 1709 first has secured authors by law to authorize the production or reproduction of literary, dramatic, musical, and artistic works and has granted the sole right for a period of 14 years. The act also decrees that the copyright has to remain with the authors for additional 14 years if leaving.

The United States Constitution in 1787 has empowered Congress, to promote the progress of science and useful arts by securing or limited times to authors the exclusive rights to their respective writings and discoveries. The copyright act in United State has been passed in 1790 which follows the British precedents for the period of copyright to the authors *i.e.* 14 years plus 14 years with renewal possibilities.[1]

The French Republican Constitution has stated the copyright issue on 3rd September 1791 thus: "Authors of any kind of written works, music composers, painters and drawing artists who may pictures and drawings, are to enjoy an exclusive life long right to sell their works, to put them for sale to diffuse them through out the territory of the Republic and to determine to whom they belong as a whole or in part".[2]

2. The Berne Convention

The progress of country-wise legislation on copyright has not enough to solve the problem of international editorial and literary piracy and hence the international movement of copyright has started by the late 19th Century. The first international conference on copyright has been held on 9th September 1886 in Berne. In this famous Brene Convention, the International Association for the Protection of Authors over Literary and Artistic Works has established. This Convention has been modified and amended another six times for the present: in Paris (1896), in Berlin (1908), in Rome (1928), in Brussels (1948), in Stockholm (1967) and in Paris (1971). The states have signed in the Convention document which has defined in article 2 as: "Any production in the literary, scientific or artistic domain, whatever may be the mode of form of its reproduction, such as books, pamphlets, and other writings; dramatic or dramatico-musical works, choreographic works and entertainments in dumb show, the acting form of which is fixed in writing or otherwise; musical compositions with or without words; works of drawing, painting, architecture, sculpture, engraving and lithography;

illustrations, geographical charts, plans, sketches and plastic works relative to geography, topography, architecture or science. Translations, adaptations, arrangements of music and other reproductions in an altered form of a literary or artistic work, as well as collections of different works, shall be protected as original works without prejudice to the rights of the author of original works"[3].

Brene Convention has provided copyright protection for life term of the author plus 50 years after author's expiry. The Convention has made the provision for longer term of copyright protection according to the discretion of national governments. Thus the copyright expiry varies country to country. An international poll has taken in 1975, which shows that the shortest period of '*post mortem auctoris*' (after author's death) is applied in the USSR (15 years). The period of post mortem auctoris varies country to country like thus: Peru (20 years), Liberia, Mexico, Poland, Salvador (25 years), Bolivia, China, Korea, Japan, Philippines, Sweden, etc. (30 years), Uruguay (40 years). In most countries, Argentina, Australia, Burma, Canada, Denmark, France, Germany, Great Britain, Indonesia, Ireland, Israel, Lebanon, Netherlands, New Zealand, South Africa, Sri Lanka, Switzerland, Turkey, etc., it is applied for 50 years. It expires after 60 years in Brazil, 80 years in Colombia and Panama, and never expires in Portugal. Presently, in Europe and USA the period of copyright protection for original work is life term of the author plus 70 years after his/her death. In India, authors enjoy copyright protection during lifetime plus 60 years after death.

3. The Indian Copyright Law

India Government has enacted Copyright Act in the year 1957 and that has amended five times in 1981, 1984, 1992, 1994 and 1999. The 1999 amendment of Indian Copyright Act has the full compatibility with Trade Related Aspects of Intellectual Property Rights (TRIPS) agreement. Indian Copyright, under chapter 3, provides the legal protection for different categories which are :

(*a*) Original literary works, for *e.g.* novels, instruction manual, computer programme, lyric for song, article in news paper, some type of databases.

(*b*) Original dramatic work, including works of dance or mime.

(*c*) Original musical works.

(*d*) Original artistic works *e.g.* paintings, engravings, photographs, sculptures, collages, works of architecture, technical drawing, diagrams, maps, logos.

(*e*) Published edition of works *e.g.* typographical arrangement of a publication.

(*f*) Sound recording, which may be recordings of any medium *e.g.* tape or compact disk and may be recording of others copyright works *e.g.* musical or literary.

(*g*) Films including videos.

(*h*) Broadcast and cable programmes.

(*i*) Pantomimes and choreographic works; and

(*j*) Architectural works.[4]

The Indian Copyright Act, 1957 as amended in 1999 has twelve chapters. Chapter 11 lists out acts e.g. reproduction of literary, dramatic, musical and artistic works in the form of cinematograph film without license or permission by the copyright owner shall be deemed to be copyright infringement.

4. Library and Copyrighted Materials

Libraries are storehouse of copyrighted materials of past and present knowledge or work. Libraries have been established with the intention that they should acquire huge quantity of documents, information materials; store them in such a scientific way that they can be retrieved as and when required by the users or members of the library.

Libraries since long have been performed one pivotal role in the society for realizing right to knowledge to the individuals of the society. Human creatively acts as boosting up the condition of the society or social cultural process. Library documents or collections are the crucial resource of cultural heritage for the information society, from which all kinds of human creativity get primary and raw materials. Innovetions are developed as continuity from the past or reaction to that. Library through its collection play a significant role in the distribution of information.

5. Library : The Non-Profit Service Organization

Libraries are basically service organization having the documents or information which acquired through purchase, complementary as their own. But the problem of libraries remains otherwise; they do not have the materials as their sole, for the copyright of the materials hold by the authors/ publishers of that acquired materials / information. Therefore, libraries are not free to cater effective information service or library services to its clientele, though most of libraries are established and maintained with public funds. They are maintained in the belief that people should have access to this knowledge storage and by using that information a citizen will be a better citizen. Therefore, libraries are engaged to extend the boundaries of human knowledge. Generally, libraries are operated for the people without charging any fees for their service and so libraries are non-profit organization.

6. Variety Library Clientele and Their Use

Each and every library has various types of its clientele and they use the library in various way. The user of library books or documents may be just a casual reader who are transfer his recreation or may be a student or researcher who may take notes from those as part of learning process or preparing research paper. Likewise historians, literary critics, journalists, scientists, doctors and other must borrow books and to have handy information and thus developing new generation knowledge.

7. Problems Regarding Library Services

To serve its clientele librarian has to face some problems due to Copyright law, which protects the copyrighter owner against the unauthorized reproduction of copies and their sale in market. The copyright holders may impose restrictions for the use of copyrighted books thus :

1. "All right reserved. No part of this book may be reproduced or utilized in any form or by any means, electronic or mechanical, including photocopying, recording or by any information storage or retrieval system, without permission in writing from the publisher."

2. "For copyright reasons this book may not be issued to the public on loan or otherwise except in its original soft cover." In normal practice libraries bought books, stored or displayed them for the readers. Readers may look / read books with normal vision, or by using glasses, magnifying glasses, microscopes, mirrors, television, computers etc. Readers may lend those for home use taking out from library. Readers may use coping method such as note taking or even they may request the Librarian for photocopying. It would be impossible to the Librarian to refrain readers from using coping methods, even if it were illegal in the light of copyright law.[5]

8. Problem Solving Action Taken by the Librarians and Other Organizations

Realizing the serious problems of librarians for catering proper library services to the clientele, some actions have been taken by the Library Associations, International Organizations and Courts.

8.1 : International Library Loan

Librarians have always received queries/requests for information or document from the internal institutional members, where the library exists, and supply the required information/document from internal resources. The librarian may also receive queries which may not be supplied from his/ her own resources and for that he/she have to loan documents from other institutes, within the country or outside the country. This type of loan system has been accepted by international law.

"Libraries have been subject to international law since the Brussels Convention of 1886, which concerned the exchange of public documents and publications of scientific and literary societies, and was the first international library agreement". The concept of international library loan has grown as the International Library Committee adopts rules for international book lending in 1936; new rules have been elaborated in 1954. The UNESCO has taken drive for international library cooperation since 1948.[6]

8.2 : Copyright and Library Association

The problem of photocopying of library documents has long been the subject of discussion among the Publishers Association and Library Association. In American Library Association report 1964 pointed out the following :

"1. The making of a single copy by a library is a direct and natural extension of traditional library service.

2. Such service, employing modern coping methods, has become essential.

3. The present demand can be satisfied without inflicting measurable damage on Publishers and copying processes will not materially affect the demand for single copy library duplication for research purpose".[7]

8.3 : The Doctrine of Fair Use

Copyright law is silent on library copying. A doctrine of 'fair use' has been developed partly through court decisions, partly through actual practice followed in libraries since the beginning of library system and partly through cooperative efforts between Librarians and Publishers.

The doctrine of fair use has developed through distillation of court decisions for maintaining some balance between the copyrighted document and its users. The fair use doctrine permits the reproduction of copyrighted work by considering the factors :

(*a*) The purpose and character of use;

(*b*) the nature of copyrighted work;

(*c*) the amount and substantiality of the portion used in relation to the copyrighted work as a whole; and

(*d*) the effect of the use upon the potential market for or value of the copyrighted work.[8]

8.4 : Copyright Act

The Indian Copyright Act, 1957 as amended in 1999 permits the user of making use of any copyrighted materials without the prior permission of the copyright holder for the five reasons :

1. Single copy for private, personal or non-commercial use– research and study,
2. teaching,
3. quotations,
4. criticism or review and
5. judicial proceedings.[9]

Regarding library reprographic services, the Act provision is quite revealing and in chapter it is stated that "the making of not more than three copies of the book (including a pamphlet, sheet of music, map, chart or plan) by or under the direction of a person in charge of a public library for the use of the library, if such book is not available for sale in India".[10]

9. Digital Library

Now the library has entered into digital era by the advent of Information and communication technology. Libraries are engaged to develop their digital collection to meet the multifarious need of the academicians and researchers apart from the existing physical printed collections. The types of procurement of digital collections of libraries are : (*a*) in physical format – cassettes, floppies, CDs, DVDs etc. and (*b*) in accessible format – e-books, bibliographical databases, e-journals etc. The use of these digital information materials/sources has protected by copyright law. The Digital Millennium Copy Right Act, 1988 adapted by US Congress in the most comprehensive reform of copyright law. In India, Information Technology Act, 2000 provides a framework for legal recognition of electronic communication, storage of electronic data, licensing of cyber organization, etc., which is amended in the year 2008.

10. Conclusion

Copyright issues leads to increase unease among the librarians and the library community people because those are procuring digital or non-digital collections and providing services out of those materials. The problem of libraries is really high because they are simply caretakers of information and not own the copyright of materials they hold in their stock. Copyright is an exclusive right conferred by the

Government to the creator of knowledge. Again, library collects that knowledge for the citizens of that Government for making them good citizens.

But these services of libraries are not clearly permitted by the law; hence librarians feel shaky and hesitate for catering proper services. Lastly, the demand for necessary amendment is quite justified that copyright law should be clear, specific and understandable and on the basis of that librarian may be guided and involved in their noble profession to execute their service effectively and efficiently. It is required because libraries have always acquired resources to meet the demand and needs of its clientele.

References

1. Encyclopaedia of Library and Information Science, Volume 6. New York : Marcel Dekker, 1971.
2. Osmanczyk, E.J. : The Encyclopedia of United Nations and International Agreements. 2nd. Ed. New York: Taylor and Francis, 1990.
3. *Ibid.*, p. 96.
4. Narayana, P. : Intellectual property law. Kolkata: Eastern Law House, 1999. [As referred by Das, Jaba : Copyright and Library. *In* Knowledge Management in Special Libraries in Digital Environment: XXIV All India Conference of IASLIC, Dehradun, 2003. p. 255-260.].
5. Encyclopedia of Library and Information Science. *op. cit.*
6. Osmanczyk, E.J. *op.cit.*
7. Encyclopedia of Library and Information Science, *op. cit.* p. 95.
8. *Ibid.*
9. Singh, DharamVeer and Malik, Babita : Rights and issues of copyright and library materials. *In* Knowledge organisation in digital environment in libraries (KODEL) : Introspects and prospects : ILA Golden Jubilee Conference Papers, Vadodara, 2004. p. 608-618.
10. Raju, A.A.N. A Look into important provisions of the Indian Copyright Act, 1957. *In* National bibliographical control: problems and perspectives: essays for A.K. Dasgupta. Kolkata: Allied, 2003. p. 76-83.

Chapter 11

Library and Electronic Recording Technology (ERT)

Recently one important change has taken place in library field, which has changed the environment of the library, *i.e.* Electronic Recording Technology (ERT) or digitization technology media and its dominancy in society. Library has also welcomed this new system, as it is not out of the society. Moreover, librarians and its parent institutions have realized that this ERT is a boon for the library. And by the help of this ERT, librarian will be able to invite more confidently its clientele as before. So many Libraries and Information Centres are engaged to use ERT for their existing documents and to serve their clientele.

1. Environmental Changes in University Libraries

The need for education and research of any university is always highly dependant on its library. But it is impossible to procure all the necessary documents/data/information even for any single subject in any university as the growth of information/publication in any subject is going on very high speed and in multifarious media technology.

Knowledge is rapidly expanding, even in any particular subject, in the proliferation of books and other documents *i.e.*, newsletters, magazines and journals etc. on the topic/subject. The sheer volume of these materials has made storing and accessing them a major and increasingly expensive task for libraries through out the world. Space limitations are one constraint; accessing the information is another. A very common demand from academic departments is that major journals of different subjects must be subscribed to, and provision should be there to consult those journals individually into the library.

But to face the demands of modern readers soon it is realized that this manual system is not sufficient. To face the demands of users, university librarians have introduced automation, a new environment to his/her library. Librarian has taken initiative to serve his/her clientele in two ways : (1) from the internal resources of the library and (2) from the external resources. Therefore, a new environment has been developed in a university library where users demand for new knowledge generated anywhere in the world.

For this environmental changes the university librarian should note or emphasize the important phenomena like: technical expertise; visit of other library that have already accepted the scheme; and specifying proposed area to be covered or what will be the first choice for the site or library. And it is true that it would be too expensive to switch over the traditional library to digital library.

2. Electronic Recording Technology (ERT)

The Electronic Recording Technology (ERT) has provided alternative to the traditional methods and procedure of recording human knowledge including primitive knowledge. It has enabled to record human knowledge in better way, in digitized form. The ERT system captures print records in such a way that they have exact contents, context and structure. So digitized records from print media are authentic, authoritative, reliable and purposeful. The advantage of digitized media record is that it remained available, understandable and usable for long period.

To start the ERT system in the library, some basic components are required for the organization where a digital library is to be attached / augmented. These components are as under :

(*a*) Local Area Network (LAN).

(*b*) Nodes connected with computers (PCs).

(*c*) Stable Server to store huge information/knowledge.

(*d*) CD-Rom Collections and CD-Drive.

(*e*) Multimedia Kit.

(*f*) Internet facilities.

(*g*) Speedy Communication System.

(*h*) E-mail, Fax, Voice Message services.

(*i*) Manpower with sound computer knowledge.

(*j*) Software for operation and searching.

(*k*) Printer, Scanner, Copier, etc.

Necessary Hardware : (*a*) Server, (*b*) PC, (*c*) Scanner, (*d*) Camera, (*e*) CD Writer, (*f*) Storage media *e.g.* CD; DVD; Hard Disk; Juke Box CDH to load more CD at a time; CD Server.

Necessary Software : (*a*) Operating System (OS); (*b*) Scanners having software in built. For detailed bibliographic information, indexing of scanning items/images and their retrieval purposes Optical Character Recognition (OCR) method is used to scan. Although for old documents many other scanning/image solutions software are available in the market, viz. VISUAL; Data Scan; Omni Page; Q Series; Tech Lib; GEAC, etc.

3. ERT Process

Librarian can use scanning methods for digitizing his internal old and rare documents. For this purpose several scanners have to be used depending the nature and type of original document. To scan documents scanner's resolution is very important. High resolution affects the level of details of image of the original document. Presently the scanning resolution varies from 200 to 600 dpi (dot per inch).

Another thing is important for the image that is its colour. It depends on number of pixels, which are small cells or blocks of tones. Normally we have three methods; 1-bit or Bi-toned, Gray Scale Image and Colour Image on which the colour of the image of a document depends.

The quality of scanner is measured by the number pixels per unit. Most scanners can read at least 300 dots per inch. More dots mean better resolution: finer lines and sharper pictures/images.

3.1 : Image Acquisition Processing

Imaging is one of the ERT processes, which has several steps from original document to digital image form.[1] All these steps are to be found in the figure 1.

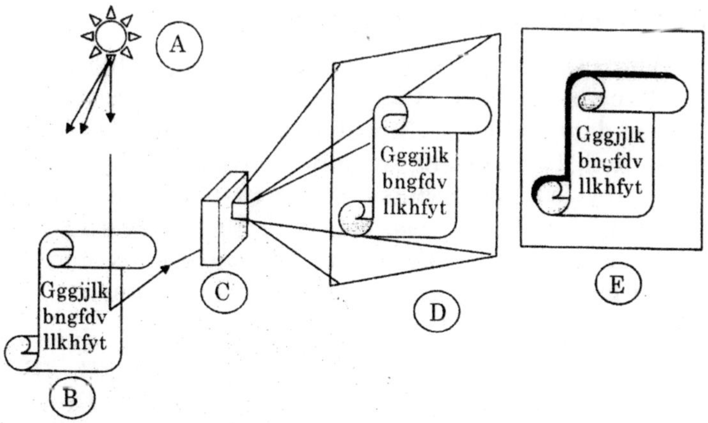

Fig. 1 : An example of Digital Image Acquisition Process.

Notes : A = Energy (illumination) source; B = Scene element (Library manuscript); C = Imaging system (scanner, etc.); D = Image plane (Library manuscript); E = Digital Image (Library manuscript).

From the stated figure we may get the idea how conversions of a library document, say manuscript, into digital image forms by the help of ERT. The figure shows that the energy has been transmitted from an illumination source as "A", and that is being reflected from a scene element *i.e.* manuscript (library document) as noted here "B". This energy could also be transmitted through the scene element (library manuscript). Now the imaging system, which is shown as "C", has to perform two functions: to collect the incoming energy and focus it onto an image plane as we mark here "D". Here, the illumination is light and the front end of the imaging system is a lens, which projects the viewed scene onto the lens focal plane. Now the sensor array, which is coincident with the focal plane, produces output proportional to the integral of the light received at each sensor. Digital and analog circuitry sweeps these outputs and converts them to a video signal, which is then digitized by another section of imaging system.

Thus we get the output of a digital image of the manuscript (library document), as shown in "E". Thus, after getting individual image one by one, computer itself generates and stores these images into computer as ERT files.

3.2 : ERT Files and Recommended Formats

Data can be digitized in a text file, image, audio, video or multimedia process. A number of bytes are required to represent data and for multimedia data huge number of bytes are required. To represent digitally 1 second of video requires 160 megabytes. Two minutes of CD quality music requires more than 84 millions bytes. Therefore, the high capacities of storage device techniques are to be required to store the digitized image, audio, video and multimedia data.

Some commonly used image compression techniques are: CALIS, DMC, JPEG, JPEG-LS, JPEG 2000, MPEG, JBIG, JBIG-2, GIF, LBG, PDF, Photo CD, TIFF, CCITT Group 4, Hoffman Coding, etc.

The universally accepted formats for various types of files that are related to ERT are noted in table 1.

Table 1 : File formats relating to ERT

Serial No.	*File Types*	*Universally accepted formats/Standards for representing the file*
1.	Text	ASCII (.txt), DOC (.doc), PDF (.pdf), HTML, SGML
2.	Image	CGM (.cgm), GIF (.gif), JPEG (.jpg), TIFF (.tif), BMP (.bmp), PGM (.pgm), PPM (.ppm)
3.	Audio	AIF (.aif), MIDI (.midi), MP3, MPEG-2 (.mpg), WAV (.wav), SND (.snd)
4.	Video	MPEG-1 and MPEG-2 (.mpg), Apple Quick Time (.mov)
5.	Multimedia	Auto CAD (.dxf), Adobe Photoshop, Flash.

Libraries have many old and rare documents to be digitized in the new environment therefore, the question of space for storage is also came in front automatically. The solutions are also readily available for librarians, if they accept the data compression method to store their digitized documents.

3.3 : Data Compression

Data compression is one of the enabling technologies to put image, audio, video and multimedia in computers. Data compression, according to K Sayood[2], is the art or science of representing digitized information in a compact form. By using data compression the digitized data again restructured. The total process may be represented thus in figure 2.

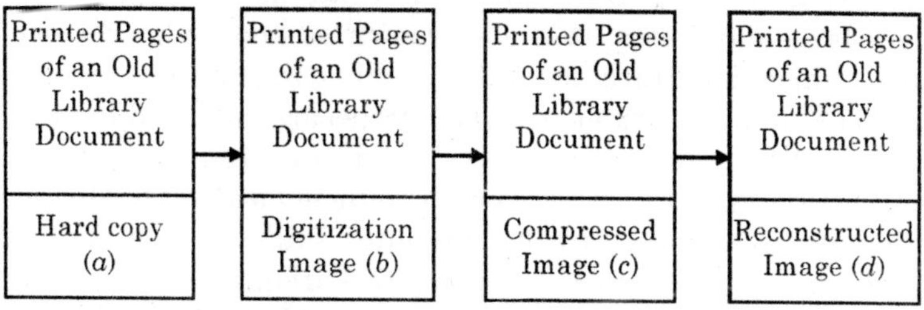

Figure 2 : Application of Data Compression on old printed library documents

From the example of compression technique in figure 2, it may be clear about the Compression Schemes, we have library documents in print version as (*a*). This (*a*) scanned as an exact copy of original printed document and called as digitized image (*b*). By using compression scheme this (*b*) can be compressed and thus we can have the compressed image (*c*). And, this compressed image involves with some restructuring process and finally, converted as reconstructed image (*d*). If we follow the lossy scheme of compression then (*d*) will be different from [b], but if we take the help of lossless scheme of compression this (*d*) will be identical to (*b*). It is obvious that lossless scheme of compression is much better relating to digitize and compression of old library document as it represents the original documents identical.

The data compression schemes are of two types : (*i*) Lossy Compression Scheme and (*ii*) Lossless Compression Scheme. In Lossy Compression Scheme it involves some loss of data/images, which are compressed and so data/images cannot be recovered or reconstructed exactly. In case of Lossless Compression Scheme data/image are compressed without loss of information and the original data/images can be recovered or reconstructed exactly from the compressed data/images.

Now the question will naturally come how we will retrieve these compressed data? With the help of data mining and optical character recognition it can be solved automatically.

3.4 : Data Mining

In the word of Bigus[3] "Data mining is the efficient discovery of valuable, non obvious information from a large collection of data". Data mining is a method of search from very large databases. It is also known as knowledge discover tool, which identifies the relationships in data. It includes tasks of knowledge extension, data archeology, data exploration, data pattern processing, data dredging, and information harvesting. All this activities are conducted automatically and allow quick discovery to the computer skilled person as well as the non-programmer. According to Turban & Aronson[4], the following are the major characteristics and objectivities of the data mining :

- Data are often buried deep within very large databases, which sometimes contain data from several years. In some cases, data are consolidated in a data warehouse.
- The data mining environment is usually that of a client/server architecture.
- The miner is often an end user, empowered by data drills and other query tools to ask ad-hock questions and obtain answers quickly with little or no programming skill.
- Data mining tools are easily combined with spreadsheets and other software development tools. Thus, the mined data can be analyzed and processed quickly and easily.

3.5 : Optical Character Recognition (OCR)

Optical character Recognition (OCR) is a machine process that turns visible alphanumeric signs into coded data according to the standard pattern of recognition. OCR system scans data and produce an image of the input item or page or document and use to convert the scanned image into the corresponding ASCII code, *i.e.* the code by which the computer processes textual information or file.

Scanners are of several types: small hand-hold scanners which can be used to read a few rows of dots at one time. Flat-bed scanners are those, which scan the entire page automatically and store that page as an image in a file of computer. Scanner also can be used to input text and data into computer. Scanners first converts the page into a picture of dots, then OCR software examines picture and looks for text. The OCR software checks each line and deciphers one character at a time. OCR can convert handwriting to computer text. It also can convert typed characters to computer text. It is obviously true that deciphering individual handwriting is much more difficult than reading typed characters for OCR software.[5] Still it is very much needed to use camera added panel based scanner with OCR software for ERT and purpose of digitizing the old and rare library documents, and Manuscripts. Actually, this type of scanner can take images ranging 2×A4 pages to 2×A2 pages.

4. Librarians Role

In the new library environment, librarians have no doubt a great and fundamental role. It is the primary motto of a librarian to serve his clientele pin-pointedly, expeditiously and exhaustively. The working Librarians should have the proper knowledge of Information and Communication Technology (ICT), acquired it beforehand to enter into the Library Profession should be updated. For the planning and supervision of ERT, some knowledge on ICT is most essential. And for that, he should know the new dimension of the different areas of Information and Communication Technology, basic media technology and tools required for the purpose and IT based library working processes which stated in Table 2.

5. Conclusion

In conclusion it may said that digital encoding as patterns of bits represents the database texts, images, graphics, and sounds. The librarian should keep in his mind in creation of local database that it will be presentable on the World Wide Web and therefore, he must accept one of the standards, *i.e.*, ASCII, Unicode, JPEG, TIFF, WAV and MP3 as these allow for the encoding, storage, exchange, and decoding of multimedia information of database.

Table 2 : Area of Information and Communication Technology (ICT), Basic Media Technology and Tools Required for the IT Based Library Working Processes.

Area of Information and Communication Technology	*Basic media technology and tools*	*IT based Library working process*
Document Storage devices	CD-ROM, Data base, E-book, E-journal, etc.	Proper Staking/ storage of knowledge.
Documents Processing.	PC, Disk driver, CD-ROM driver, Scanner, Data base, etc.	Computer Acquisition, Processing, Circulation, Reference, Periodical, & Documentation Work.
Equipments	PC, LAN, Printer, Scanner, CD writer, Barcode Scanner, Telephone with Internet, Fax and E-mail connectivity, Library software, etc.	Media and equipment handling knowledge
Clientele Approach	On-line search through Terminals and INTERNET	Understanding of intra-library LAN, terminals and INTERNET
Delivery of Documents	Physical and On-line searching Hard Copy, E-copy, through E-mail, Fax, Internet, etc.	Skill of searching e-books & e-journals, data bases, and handling e-mail, Fax, Internet, etc.
Library Personnel	Skill for computer operation in changed ERT environment	Training; Orientation; Self Learning; PC Operation for Library House Keeping Jobs.

A new horizon has been opened before librarians for acquisition, preservation and storage, and retrieval of old, rare, fragile documents and non-book materials, specially manuscripts those were in his/her holdings since long back. Librarian can digitize those documents with the help of ERT system. It is also important to note that the service normally rendered by the librarian to its clientele will be more qualitative and accurate if this ERT system accepted to the particular library. So, we can conclude by saying that ERT system enriches the skill of librarians and capable him/her to provide effective library service to the users circle.

References

1. Gonzalez, R.C. and Woods, R.E. : Digital image processing. 2nd. Ed. Delhi: Pearson Education, 2003.
2. Sayood, K. : Introduction to data compression. 2nd. Ed. New Delhi: Harcourt India, 2000.
3. Bigus, J.P. : Data mining with neural networks. New York: McGraw Hill, 1996. [As cited by Turban, E. and Aronson, J.E.: Decision support systems and intelligent systems. $6^{th.}$ ed. Delhi: Pearson Education Asia, 2001. p.148.].
4. Turban, E. and Aronson, J.E. : Decision support systems and intelligent systems. $6^{th.}$ ed. Delhi: Pearson Education Asia, 2001.
5. Post, G.V. and Anderson, D.L. : Management information systes: solving business problems with information technology. New Delhi: Tata McGraw Hill, 1998.

Chapter 12

Managing University Library in Changing Environment

Libraries are the storehouse of recorded human knowledge, which are of different types *i.e.* books, manuscripts, maps, reports, patents, microfiches, microfilms, etc. These physical objects of recorded human knowledge are of different subjects, different times, different ages, different lingual, different countries, and that have different medium of recording but arranged scientifically. It is true that men are using different items in different times for their recording of knowledge. It is also true that men are using different medium for their knowledge recording. All these changes have a history, which is always be remembered by the librarians as the organization and management of libraries have always been influenced by this change. The library that has several items of human knowledge is beyond the traditional library and should be handled in different way and in complex manner.

Now-a-days most of the modern university libraries have all the items together in its collection. So it is a great challenge to the university librarian how efficiently he/she could manage his/her library where physical objects of the library collection are heterogeneous and library users are of varied interests. Recently university libraries have entered in an age where flow of information or searching of information have no longer been definable in geographical area or terms; but rather have international phenomena based on increased use of Information Technology and its applications and also in publications. Publishers are using communication technologies for their information products at a very increasing rate. Thus the new opportunities have been created in the field of library and information system which influences for taking some positive changes in pattern of providing library services in universities.

1. Changing Environment in University Libraries

The three new approaches–technological changes, library authority's changed outlooks and changed pattern of Government's support – have forced to establish the transac-tional network system in university libraries. With the help of this network, university libraries could reach or avail huge number of information resources particularly e-resources and by using these e-resources librarians have to serve the library clientele.

Now, the trends of collection, storage, retrieval system of libraries and institutions have been changed. Scientists and scholars working in research organizations are always expecting information with very high speed. This demand has two influences :

1. Data, information, document should be created or published as quick as possible, and
2. that resources should be available to the scientists or scholars as soon as they have generated.

2. Changes in E-Resources Publishing

Libraries are always procuring documents for building its resources. Now, the first change or influence goes to publishers – who are now publishing e-documents along with print documents with a very high speed. The big companies or enterprises have been using advanced means of communication system and spread their activities across the globe with their new flexible e-products of information. These enterprises have influenced on the behaviour of university librarians regarding e-resource collection development and library procurement policy all over the World. Recently a good numbers of e-resources enterprises or publishers have come out with huge number of electronic resources.

2.1 : Types of E Resources and Their Users

Several publishers have shown their interest for e-publishing as the pattern of information seeking organization and behaviour of clientele have rapidly changed due to influence of Information Technology and Computer Technology with the applications of recently developed hardware and software. E-resources that are published by the publishers as under :

(*a*) ***CD-ROMs*** : CD-ROMs are chief e-resources available in the market and accepted as major e-resource for university libraries. Large amount of data stored in it, which can be retrieved off-line or on-line with user-friendly search software.

(*b*) ***E-Journals*** : E-journals are the electronic version of print journals, which is now available as electronic full-text on-line. These e-journals are available on subscription basis for the university libraries and easy to search by the library clientele.

(*c*) ***Abstracting and Indexing Databases*** : Like abstracting and indexing journals electronic abstracting and indexing databases are available for the library, which can be retrieved off-line or on-line.

(*d*) ***E-Reports*** : Publishers are now publishing e-reports on scientific and technical innovations, which are available, on-line and act as reliable and essential resource for the scientists and researchers of any university library.

(*e*) ***E-Clippings*** : E-clippings are basically news items with date time and news source. E-clippings are available on-line and archived by the news service providers. It is a very helpful e-resource for the social science researcher.

(*f*) ***E-Content Pages*** : Publishers are now published e-content pages of books, journals, reports, manuscripts, proceedings of seminar and conferences on their website. This on-line available item of e-resource helps the scientists, researchers to gather primary information on their area of interest and may request librarians to procure the same.

(*g*) ***E-Databases*** : E-databases with bibliographical details and full-text sources are produced to meet the growing need by the researchers. These e-databases are available for the library through the web browse or through local network solutions. Some bibliographical e-databases are available in the webs which act as a helpful tool for the university librarian for acquisition of document.

(*h*) ***E-Books*** : Electronic version of printed books has become a part of e-publishing phenomenon of several publishers. A good number of e-books, almost on all subjects, are now available on the web on payment basis. Some e-books are also available on free of cost. It is now attained the hot topic of interest of Indian university librarian as one of the main e-resources for serving the need of library clientele.

Thus, one type of competition grows among the publishers, which is a great change. In the advent of electronic communication system scientists and scholars have the scope to know which publisher publishes research article within very short duration. They naturally want to expose their research invention to the world of learned people as minimum time as possible. This primary expectation of scientists and researchers has the natural impact on the publishers. Thus scopes of e-publications have been developed and the number of e-publishers has been increased day by day.

Several e-publishers have now offering different 'price packages' for the research institutions and also for university libraries. This is a changed tactics of e-publishers marketing strategy. It would be quite natural that the pricing of e-journals are to be different, and the methods of subscription systems are very much dissimilar from publisher to publisher. In this changed situation university librarians need to take lots of exercises to procure e-resources.

2.2 : E-Resources Available for Indian University Libraries

In case of creation of websites some of the e-publishers have created their websites in their original name. But some have created in different names such as Elsevier Publishing and Springer; they have used their website names as 'Science Direct' and 'Springer Link' respectively. Not all the e-publishers cover the same type of e-resources into their websites. The 'Science Direct' covers the maximum e-resource items such as: Journals, Magazines, Bibliographical databases, Abstracts, Conference Proceedings with Citation Links. Websites have been created by e-publishers on different subjects. 'Science Direct' covers the large area of Science and Technology. On the other hand, 'Project MUSE' covers the major areas of Arts, Literature, Humanities, and Social Sciences. All these details including website URLs have been revealed in Table 1.

From the table 1 it would be realized that e-publishers are now publishing variety of e-resources in different subjects. In case of pricing they are offering different price packages for the library. We may discuss here the various pricing packages offered for the e-journals, the mostly used e-resources now by the e-publishers for Indian libraries. Before going details we may discuss about the pricing policy of e-journals.

3. Changes in Pricing Pattern

The methods of pricing e-journals have stressed on some new aspects, which are changed pricing system, or different as regards to printed journals. Actually, e-journals are the knowledge content products, which are generated by a single publisher once targeting the present knowledge seekers. But the same knowledge content is always in need for future generation also. Here the customers are not limited to time and even not limited by number. The publisher takes the drive to store the same knowledge content products in archive for any future time search. So, here the price would be fair. Again, there is also the chance of monopolistic approach, as there is only one supplier of the needed goods i.e. e-knowledge content. This could happen through ownership of the single source, such as the exclusive legal protection of a patent or copyright. This is true in case of publication houses including e-Publishers. The primary aim of the e-Publisher is not only to remain in business, but to make a profit that will permit expansion and increase profits.

The price of the any print version of journal for a subscription year fixed by the publisher by calculating the actual production cost of journal issues which includes printing charges, cost of paper, cost of binding, etc. The marketing cost of the journal includes handling charges, discount to the agents for sale promotion, postage, packaging, transportation cost, etc., which are also added. The cost also considers the future development of the journal, the profit of the publisher and remuneration to the author, if any. On reviewing all these sides the price of the journal issues and the yearly subscription rate of the journal fixed. Publishers offer subscription price options considering the print price as basic price for the e-journals.

4. Changed Pricing Systems for E-Journals

Some of the world famous publishers have taken initiative to help librarians for providing electronic environment. They have created state-of-the-art IP based searching and linking functionality, and navigated via a simple and intuitive user interface. University Librarians may invest money for these e-documents as they are usually renew or subscribe print journals. Some times these e-facilities are available on the same cost, or 10% to 15% more investment. Here, the facilities have provided more then investment because, most of this type of e-access provide archives facilities for a specific period or from the very beginning of the journal, *i.e.* from volume one. If the library goes to consortium, then e-journals or databases would be available at a very low price. Some times there are packages which can be accepted as per the need and fund provision of the library.

A good university librarian has always tried to match the need of the research community and fund availability. It may be said that in this changed and new electronic environment a university librarian can be judged as successful on the basis of the utilization of library fund, to cover the research areas in progress or to estimate future possible research areas to be incorporated in his/her own research institute or university.

The e-publishing houses have now launched new price packages for the libraries. These changed pricing systems are no doubt a great environmental change in library journal procurement. Although these changed pricing systems will certainly be helpful for the librarians to procure e-resources for the libraries according to their budget. Some publishers offer following institutional subscription rate options to better meet the changed on-growing needs of the academic and research bodies or communities. Present day available subscription price options for e-journals are to be discussed here one by one.

4.1 : Combined

This subscription option includes electronic access of all contents of a particular journal for the subscription year and supply of all print issues of the same. Here yearly rate of subscription are slightly higher normally 5% than print version of the same journals.

4.2 : Combined Plus Back File

Publisher includes in this subscription option electronic access from volume one onwards of a journal and supply of print issues of that particular journal for the subscription year/volume. Here the rate of yearly subscription increases 10%-15% than print version of the same journal.

4.3 : E-Access

In this option e-access of a journal is provided excluding any supply of print issues for the subscription year. Here the rate is normally 10% less than print price of subscription year. Here e-access for a block of 5-6 years has also been provided to the institute/library with a reasonable price.

4.4 : E-Access Plus Back File

In this subscription option e-access of a journal for the subscription period as well as back files of all previous volumes of the said subscribed journal have been provided by the publisher. Here the subscription rates are only 2% to 5% higher than print subscription rates of journals.

4.5 : Back Files or Journal Archives

There is an option for Back files or Journal Archives offered by some e-journal publishers. In this option one library may access even hundred years journal archives from volume one to the present. Thus libraries can add incredible collection of research spanning more than hundred years. Publishers offer two options for Back files or Journal Archives pricing: one for annual subscription and other for permanent purchase.

4.6 : Licensing

There is an available option for an electronic-only license

for journals for the institutions and libraries. In this licensing option an institute or library can opt for single user, five users or multi users' license from the e-publisher. In licensing option packages the members of an institution or library can access e-journals through IP range. The publisher provides a unique user ID and password to the institute or library along with activation procedure. After successful activation librarian has to supply user ID and password to all of its library members. And thus each and every library member can browse those e-journals easily all through out the campus LAN on logging user ID and password. But at a time search by the reader depends on payment of license fee to the publishers.

4.7 : Consortium to Libraries

In this subscription option publishers offer all type electronic access to an apex body of any country. The concern body purchase or subscribes e-journals on behalf of the special type institutions or libraries of a country. The publishers provide IP range based e-access to the end user institutions or libraries through their e-journal website directly. If any particular library has multiple IP ranges (V-SAT, VSNL or any other Internet activity) the publishers provide e-access for their e-publication through all IP ranges.

World famous publishers those have engaged with the publication of scholarly journals earlier have also been devoted to publish e-journals to reach the scientist and scholars quickly. These e-publishers provide some pricing packages for their e-journals and other e-resources particularly for university libraries. The pricing packages of e-journals as introduced by different renowned e-publishers for the University Libraries and other libraries of Indian Research Institutions will be shown in Table 2.

From the table 2, it would be clear that in the changed pricing system, there exist seven types of different pricing models for the Indian libraries. Out of ten famous publishers, included in this discussion, all these packages have been offered by only two publishers : Elsevier Publishing and Sage publications. The other eight publishers have offered different packages for the libraries. The Oxford University Press has to

Table 1 : E-Resources Website URLs, Subject and Content Coverage Available for Indian University and other Research Institution Libraries.

E-Publishers Website Title	*E-Resource Contents/Items Covered*	*Subjects*	*Website*
ACM Digital Library	Journals, Magazines, Conference Proceedings and Bibliographical Records & E-books	Computer Sciences	http://portal.acm.org/dl.cfm
IOP Journals	Journals	Physics and Physical Sciences	www.iop.org/journals/enquiries
ASCE Journals	Journals, Periodicals and Transactions	Civil Engineering and allied subjects	www.pubs.asce.org/journals/
Science Direct	Journals, Magazines, Bibliographical databases, Abstracts, Conference Proceedings with Citation Links.	Physical, Computer, Engineering and Technological Sciences	www.sciencedirect.com
Springer Link	Journals	Science subjects	http://springerlink.com
Sage Full-text Collections	Journals with Citation Links.	Science, Humanities.	www.sagepublications.com
Project MUSE (Gateway Portal/Platform)	Journals with Citation Links and Archives of Journals, Magazines (few years back volumes)	Arts, Literature, Humanities, and Social Sciences	http://muse.jhu.edu/journals

Contd.....

E-Publishers Website Title	*E-Resource Contents/Items Covered*	*Subjects*	*Website*
Oxford University Press	Journals, Transactions, Magazines, Conference Proceedings, E-Books.	Humanities and Social Sciences	http://www.oup.com/online/
Blackwell Publishing	Journals, Abstracts, E-Books.	Humanities and Social Sciences	http://www.blackwellpublishing.com/
JSTOR (Gateway Portal/Platform)	Archives of Journals, Magazines (few years back volumes); Bibliographical databases; Abstracts; Conference Proceedings with Citation Links.	Literature, Humanities and Social Sciences	http://www.jstor.org/
Informatics	Archives of Journals (few years back volumes); Bibliographical databases; Abstracts; CD-Roms	Science, Humanities.	http://www.informindia.co.in/
Balani Infotech	Archives of Journals (few years back volumes); Bibliographical databases; Abstracts;	Science, Humanities.	http://www.balaniinfotech.com/

[*Source* : Brochure/Hard-outs/Websites Publishers]

offer only three types of packages: 'combined (print and e-access)', 'e-access' and 'back files'. All the publishers except, the Oxford University Press maintains the package 'consortia'. Six publishers offer the package 'combined plus back file' only.

Table 2 : Pricing Packages of E-Journals Offered by E-Publishers for University Libraries and Other Libraries in Indian Research Institutions.

Name of the Publishers	*Combined E-Access + Print)*	*Combined plus back file*	*E-Access*	*E-Access plus back file*	*Back files or Journal Archives*	*Licensing*	*Consortia*
IOP Publishing	√	√	–	√	√	√	√
Elsevier Publishing	√	√	√	√	√	√	√
Sage Publications	√	√	√	√	√	√	√
Springer	√	√	√	√	–	–	√
ASCE Journals	√	√	–	–	√	√	√
ACM Digital Library	√	√	–	–	√	√	√
JSTOR (Portal)	–	–	√	√	√	√	√
Project Muse (Portal)	–	–	√	√	√	√	√
Oxford University Press	√	–	√	√	–	–	–
Backwell Publishing	√	–	√	√	√	√	√
Informatics	–	–	√	√	√	√	√
Balani Infotech	–	–	–	√	√	√	√

[*Source:* Brochure/Hand-Outs/ Websites Publishers]

5. Librarian's Role in Changed Environment

From the above discussion it is found that several publishers have come out to publish e-resources *i.e.* e-books, e-journals, e-database, etc. along with their usual print resources. These e-publishers have announced several distribution packages, which are highly competitive and complex in nature and make the university librarians' e-resource procurement processes more and more complicated.

It is very much difficult to estimate by the university librarian what particular packages to be included or accepted for his/her library. There may be a chance of hidden or disguise trade practices for the particular e-resource package which remain un-exposed to the university librarian as he is not a proper businessman. Librarian may not be able to check whole package item-wise. Again, vendors or aggregators are not also sure among themselves about adulteration of e-resource packages offer, as huge numbers of e-documents are generally available in packages. There may be chances for remixing of same e-resources in the price packages, which are available, free. There are also chances of odd coverage; poor quality; inclusion of trace items, etc. All the stated factors may have added misery to the university librarians.

Actually, for procuring e-resources university librarian has to spend lot of money, effort, time and moreover he/she have to create other related infrastructure. So these e-resources should not be bad quality and on the other hand those should be dependable for the high quality education and research. Otherwise, the university librarian will definitely be questioned by the library clientele and also by the authority and that will deteriorate the condition of the library environment. To manage the situation librarian should apply two methods (*a*) 'perpetual accesses facility' and (*b*) 'consumer behaviour approach' for procuring e-resources, mainly e-journals for his/her library.

5.1 : Use the Perpetual Access Facility

Recently e-publishers or aggregators or vendors have been offered a new type proposal to university librarians that of the 'perpetual accesses' for e-journals procurement. In case of print journal, issues received under that subscription belong to the library forever. But in case of procuring e-journals some questions may come into the mind of university librarian and these are :

- If subscription is not renewed for next year for e-journals then what will happen to the earlier volumes for which the library has paid subscription?
- Do publishers provide such issues on CD-ROM, if subscription is discontinued in the next year?
- What will be the fate of e-journals for which subscription has already paid but the publisher or aggregator goes out of business?[1]

Sharon Cline McKay also shares the views on the above questions and has expressed the feelings thus: "These questions only scratch the surface of the intricately complicated issues of archiving and perpetual access. Although no clear resolution of the problems has emerged, various librarians, publishers, and aggregators are working on reaching agreements that will provide solutions". He points out thus: "all rights and permissions should be spelled out clearly in a document provided by each publishers".[2]

It is true that in this new 'perpetual accesses' approach is not usually practiced method. It is not always clearly mentioned in papers of the publishers that how long the access facility for e-journals are to be provided. The university librarian must go through all papers of the publishers/aggregators/vendors before to approve or procure e-journals for his/her library. The librarian will safe and the library would safe and sound; if 'perpetual accesses' approach is accepted for e-resources procurement.

5.2 : Use Consumer Behavour Approach

To overcome these problems university librarian may adopt 'consumer behavour approach' method[3], which attempts to emphasize the formal education on e-resources available for the library clientele. In case of university library, librarian may emphasize on demonstration programme, participating lectures, etc. It is necessary for creating awareness among the library users and subject specialists who will suggest in favour of particular e-resources or e-resource packages. This formal education on the e-resource products will create awareness and put together confidence in the minds of university library clientele and the librarian for selection of e-resources. And thus, university librarian and library clientele may fight jointly for the e-products to be acquired for their library and also pressurize jointly for the proper access of e-products procured from the e-publishers, in case of non-availability, if any.

Before going any procurement of e-resources University librarian should keep in mind the following aspects of e-resources/e-products :

(*a*) Economic aspects, *i.e.* price or cost, quality, performance capacity, coverage, etc.

(*b*) Safety aspects, *i.e.* contents of product, effects on using the same, user friendliness, etc..

(*c*) Environmental aspects, *i.e.* effects on existing infrastructure, product pollution, scarcity, etc.; and

(*d*) Legal aspects, *i.e.* mandatory requirement of branded items, provision of replacement, compensation provision, etc.

6. Conclusions

In conclusion, it may be said that as the e-resource products are new to the library and those are too costly. University librarian should be over cautious before to select those and he should think about his existing and future addition of IT infrastructure because that are most essential to manage the changed environment of the library. Acquisition of e-resources including e-journals are being relatively new trend in the information world, which may generate lot of debate over its access, storage, preservation, and copyright. But it is growing at very high rate and will soon be the most popular resource medium in university library. We are now changing the crossroad of traditional library system to computerized library system. Researchers are always interested to spare minimum time to have the information so e-resources can save the time of the readers. Thus, in university library there is a pressure from the scholars for the good stock of e-resources. It is also true this demand also estimated by the UGC, AICTE and other bodies of higher education system in our country and they have made provisions of e-resources for the libraries. In the same way service providers like DELNET, INFLIBNET, etc. are always fond of e-resources for the students, researchers, scientists, educationists and others. Only the time will tell us what shape e-resources would take in future. Its further improvement, good and bad issues surrounding it, depends much on the collaborative efforts of the publishers, librarians and researchers.

References

1. http://www.igidr.ac.in/lib/paper2.htm.

2. McKay, Sharon Cline : Accessing Electronic Journals. *Database.* April, 1999.

3. Shitole, G.Y. : Globalization and consumerism: a comparative study of India and Canada. *In* Prasad, Govind and Dutta Mishra, Anil (eds.) : Globalization: myth and reality. New Delhi: Concept, 2004. p. 308-319.

Chapter 13

Knowledge Preservation on Indigenous System of Medicine

Diseases are very much common to humankind. For the diseases and treatment we generally mean the Allopathic System, because this system is developed rapidly and used modern sophisticated instruments. So, if any one of our family members or relations ill we generally think or talk to call a doctor who practiced Allopathic System of medicine. There is no doubt that in extreme situations, the treatments devised by modern medicine can offer an unparalleled opportunity to relieved symptoms and save lives. In India, medical services are primarily the responsibility of the State Governments. The Central Government has sponsored major schemes for disease preventions and control, which are implemented nationally.

1. Origin of Indian System of Medicine

In India, from the earliest times, people have been used some plants as pain relieving. Over the centuries, Indian societies have developed its own traditions to make sense of medicinal plants and their uses. Some of these traditions and medicinal practices may seem strange and magical, others appear rational and sensible, but all of them are attempts to overcome illness and suffering, and to enhance quality of life. There are some systems of medicine originated and practiced in India in course of time. These systems are : Ayurveda, Siddha, Unani. The system Homoeopathy originated in Germany but widely practiced in India since centuries past. Some drugless therapies *viz.* Yoga and Naturopathy have been widely practiced in India long past. A large number of Indian populations, particularly those are the residents of Rural India have been using these Indigenous Systems of Medicine as oral traditions that were passed generation to generation and centuries after centuries.

2. Traditional Knowledge on Indigenous Medicine

As soon as the basis of writing method has been discovered, the oral traditions on Indigenous Systems of Medicine those are found in practice, their where abouts have been written down and codified into histories and laws. Libraries of ancient India have stored this traditional knowledge in scrolls, palm leaves, papers in a scattered manner. The system Ayurveda has a great history. "In about 400 BC, the first Ayurvedic medical school was founded by Punarvasu Atreya. He and his pupils recorded medical knowledge in treaties that would in turn influence Charaka, the scholar who is thought to have written the *Charaka Samhita*. The compendium of writings, in the form that it has come down to us, dates from around 100 AD and describes 341 plants medicines as well as medicines of animal and mineral origin. The second major work was Susruta Samhita, dating from around the same time; it displays detailed knowledge of surgery, especially plastic surgery, and is still consulted today."[1]

2.1 : Ayurveda Recognizes as Valid Medical System

This Indian traditional medicine Ayurveda has been dismissed by the then British Rulers as they believed this is mere superstition and finally in 1833 they have closed all Ayurvedic Schools and banned its practice. Thus a great Indigenous learning system of medicine fall apart and Ayurvedic knowledge retreates into villages and temples. After a century India has became a sovereign state in the year 1947, mainly some Indian physicians have began to re-evaluate Ayurveda, and thus it has regained its reputation as valid medical system.

In recent years the Ayurveda has attracted increasing attention from medical scientists through different parts of world. The World Health Organization has taken a drive "Health for All", but the organization felt that this goal cannot be achieved through the Allopathic System alone. The organization also felt that for this purpose the Indigenous

System of Medicine of different countries should be involved for the programme "Health for All". The WHO has resolved to promote its practice in developing countries.

2.2 : Other Indian Systems of Medicine

"India has 16 Agro-climate zones, 45000 different plants species and 15000 medical plants that include 7000 plants used in Ayurveda, 700 in Unani medicine, 600 in Siddha medicine and 30 in modern medicine. This makes India one among 12 mega bio-diverse countries of the world. The Indian System of Medicine have identified 1500 medicinal plants, of which 500 species are mostly used in preparation of drags. More than 150 plant species have been categorized as endangered. India, with its diversified biodiversity has tremendous potential and advantage in this emerging area. The drugs used in ISM are 90% based on plant material and are considered to be safe, cost effective and with minimal or no side effects when genuine ingredients are used. The effectiveness of these systems mainly depends upon the sustained availability of genuine raw materials. Medicinal plants are being used in preparation of medicines by registered practitioners of ISM&H, manufacture of medicines/health foods, etc. and traditional healers."[2]

3. Indian Health Programme

Now, we may look for the health programme of our country India. In India health is a state subject under the Constitution. "The Central Government's intervention to assist the State Governments is needed in the areas of control/ eradication of major communicable and non-communicable diseases, broad policy formulation, medical and para-medical education along with regularity measures, drug control and prevention of food adulteration, besides activities concerning the containment of population growth including Child Survival and Safe Motherhood (CSSM) and immunization programme".[3] It is true that Allopathic System is the prime health care programme or services or the medical facilities offered to Indian population.

Government of India and some of the State Governments have taken some measures for improving these Indigenous systems of medicine. "In post-Independence India, the Government recognized the merit of each of the Indian System of Medicine and Homoeopathy (ISM&H) and made attempts to develop them as viable systems of medicine for the health care needs of our people".[4]

Table 1 : Summary of Infrastructural Facilities Available Under Indian System of Medicine and Homoeopathy (ISM&H) as on 01.04.2001

Sl. No.	*Facilities*	*Aurveda*	*Unani*	*Siddha*	*Yoga*	*Naturo-pathy*	*Homoeo-pathy*	*Total*
1.	Hospitals	2955	312	237	7	22	307	3840
2.	Beds	43973	5128	1986	200	757	13694	65738
3.	Dispensaries	14721	958	352	65	56	7411	23563
4.	Registered Practioners $	430890	43108	17097	–	455	197252	688802
5.	(*i*) Under Graduate Colleges	196	39	2	–	6 $$	166	409
	(*ii*) Admission Capacity	7145	1410	150	–	170	9330	18205
6.	(*i*) Post Graduate Colleges #	53	5	2	–	–	17	77
	(*ii*) Admission Capacity	651	54	76	–	–	210	991
7.	Licensed Pharmacies	8386	453	384	–	–	609	9832

Figures are provisional

Note : – = Nil information; $ = Information as on 01.01.2001; $$ = These Colleges conduct 5 and half years BNYS Degree Course; # = All these Colleges are part of U.G. Colleges mentioned at Sl. No. 5(*i*) except two Colleges under Ayurveda one each in Gujrat and West Bengal where only P.G. Courses are conducted; As such total number of Colleges under Ayurveda comes to 198. However, total number of Colleges under Unani, Siddha and Homoeopathy remain 39, 2, and 166 respectively.

[***Source :*** India. Ministry of Health and Family Welfare. Department of ISM and Homoeopathy. *Indian Systems of Medicine and Homoeopathy in India* 2001. New Delhi, 2002 (p. 21) with some modifications.]

Presently, separate Directorates of Indian System of Medicine and Homoeopathy (ISM&H) has been established in most of the States, *viz.* Andhra Pradesh, Arunachal Pradesh, Assam, Bihar, Goa, Gujrat, Hariyana, Himachal Pradesh, Jammu and Kasmir, Karnataka, Kerala, Madhya Pradesh, Maharastra, Manipur, Meghalaya, Orrisa, Punjab, Rajasthan, Tamil Nadu, Tripura, Uttar Pradesh, and West Bengal. Some of the Union Territories have taken Indian System of Medicine and Homoeopathy (ISM&H) programme, *viz.* Andaman and Nicobar Islands, Chandigarh, Delhi, Lakshadweep and Pondicherry.

In 1995, the Union Government established a separate Department under Ministry of Health and Family Welfare which may be treated as a major achievement for the Indian System of Medicine, *i.e.* Ayurveda, Yoga and Naturopathy, Unani, Siddha and Homoeopathy. The Department is renamed as Ayurveda, Yoga and Naturopathy, Unani, Siddha and Homoeopathy (AYUSH) from November, 2003. From the table-1 it may be estimated the facilities that are offered by the Government in favour of the Indian System of Medicine and Homoeopathy (ISM&H). Table-2 will show statewise population, ISM + H registered doctors and their ratio over population throughout the country.

Table 2 : Number of ISM & H Doctors (Registered Practitioners, IQ + NIQ) per 10000 population as on 1.1.1999

Sl. No.	*States/U.T.'s*	*Total Population (as per 1991 Census) $*	*ISM & H Doctors Registered Practitioners IQ + NIQ*	*ISM & H Doctors Per 10000*
1	*2*	*3*	*4*	*5*
1.	Andhra Pradesh	66508008	27944*	4.2
2.	Arunachal Pradesh	864558	–	–
3.	Assam	22414322	714#	0.3
4.	Bihar	86374465	104630#	12.1
5.	Delhi	9420644	10650	11.3
6.	Goa	1169793	–	

(Contd...)

1	*2*	*3*	*4*	*5*
7.	Gujarat	41309582	20225	4.8
8.	Haryana	16463648	25873	15.7
9.	Himachal Pradesh	5170877	8328	16.1
10.	Jammu & Kashmir@	7718700	505 #	0.6
11.	Karnataka	44977201	17173	3.8
12.	Kerala	29098518	22240	7.6
13.	Madhya Pradesh	66181170	54353	8.2
14.	Maharashtra	78937187	76728	9.7
15.	Manipur	1837149	–	–
16.	Meghalaya	1774778	229	1.3
17.	Mizoram	689756	–	–
18.	Nagaland	1209546	–	–
19.	Orissa	31659736	8401	2.7
20.	Punjab	20281969	32790	16.1
21.	Rajasthan	44005990	31880	7.2
22.	Sikkim	406457	–	–
23.	Tamil Nadu	55858946	31932	5.7
24.	Tripura	2757205	–	–
25.	Uttar Pradesh	139112287	92595	6.7
26.	West Bengal	68077965	43907	6.4
27.	A & N Islands	280661	–	–
28.	Chandigarh	642015	316	4.9
29.	D & N Haveli	138477	–	–
30.	Daman & Diu	101586	–	–
31.	Lakshadweep	51707	–	–
32.	Pondicherry	807785	–	–
	Total	**846302688**	**611413**	**7.2**

Figures are provisional.

Note : IQ = Institutionally Qualified, NIQ = Non-institutionally Qualified, - = Nil information, * = Information is available for one Board only, @ = 1991 Census was not held in Jammu & Kashmir. The figures are as per projections prepared by the Standing Committee of experts on Population Projection, October, 1989. $ = Source : Registrar General of India. # = No information has been received for the current year hence repeated for the latest available year.

[***Source :*** www.indiamedicine.nic.in]

4. Preservation of ISM Knowledge

Government has taken some steps to preserve ISM knowledge. Keeping in view the increasing popularity of traditional systems of medicine, the demand of these medicinal plants is poised to grow more. Therefore, it is needed to take some steps to increase their availability throughout the country where possible. Finally, the need for preservation of ISM knowledge is essential.

4.1 : Formation of Medicinal Plants Board

Thus the Medicinal Plants Board has been set up under the Government resolution notified in November 14, 2000 under the chairmanship of the Minister of Union Health & Family Welfare. It is a national level nodal body, which has been established to formulate a policy for conservation, harvesting, research and development, marketing of medicinal plants[5]. Some of the chief functions are identified as :

1. Acting as co-operating agency with Ministries/ Departments/Organisations/State/UT Governments for development of medicinal plants in general.
2. Acting as advisory body and provide guidance in formulation of proposals, schemes and programmes, etc. for cultivation, collection, storage and transportation of medicinal plants.
3. Identification, inventorisation and quantification of medical plants.
4. Undertaking Research and Development Studies.
5. Awarding Scientific, Technological research and Cost effective studies.
6. Development of protocols for cultivation and quality control.
7. Encouraging the Protection of Patent Rights and IPR.
8. Setting up of database system for inventorisation, dissemination of information and facilitating the prevention of Patents being obtained for medicinal use of plants, which is in the public domain.

4.2 : Publications/Documentation on Standards, Formularies, etc.

Pharmacopoeia Committees of Ayurveda, Siddha, Unani and Homoeopathy set up by the Government. Committees are engaged in involving the standards of drags. 32 laboratories of reputed Universities/Institutes and Pharmacopoeial Laboratory for Indian Medicine and Homoeopathic Pharmacopoeia Laboratory are working together for the purpose of standardization of ISM drugs. Pharmacopoeial standards for 45 Unani and 258 Ayurveda drags have already been established. Homoeopathy Pharmacopoeia Committee has evolved standards for 916 drags contained in eight volumes.

The essential lists of 636 Ayurvedic, 746 Unani and 248 Siddha drugs with formularies have been published. The Department of ISM and Homoeopathy have prepared and essential drag list for stocking these medicines to the hospitals and dispensaries of ISM and Homoeopathy. This essential list of drags is also helpful to guide the State Governments and other organizations to stock these Indigenous medicines which are frequently required for the treatment of people under the ISM and Homoeopathy

4.3 : Digitization on Indigenous System of Medicine

Some efforts from Government Departments have been taken very recently to digitize the documents on Indian System of Medicine and Homoeopathy (ISM&H). Recently, the Ministry of Health & Family Welfare, Government of India has decided to record the traditional knowledge of Indigenous system of medicine, which have been practiced centuries past in India and which remain scattered throughout India.

In order to prevent drug claims on traditional (ISM and H) medicines a database of about 35000 formulations contained in original texts of Ayurveda is being prepared under Traditional Knowledge Digital Library (TKDL)[6] project in collaboration with Council of Scientific and Industrial Research (CSIR), Experts from the different disciplines, *i.e.* Ayurveda, Information Technology, Patent and Intellectual Property Rights are engaged in this Project. About 16000 formulations have been covered so far within this Project.

Currently the Ministry of Health and Family Welfare has taken a collaborative contract project for the Department of Ayurveda, Yoga and Naturopathy, Unani, Siddha and Homoeopathy (AYUSH), on Traditional Knowledge Digital Library (TKDL) under the guidance and direct supervision of National Institute of Science Communication and Information Resources (NISCAIR), an unit of Council of Scientific Industrial Research. The Department Indian System of Medicine and Homoeopathy (ISM&H) has now changed its name as the Department of Ayurveda, Yoga and Naturopathy, Unani, Siddha and Homoeopathy (AYUSH).

4.4 : Database Creation

In order to create computerized databases, the Government of India has established National Information System on Science and Technology (NISSAT) under the Department of Scientific and Industrial Research. The National Information Centre Drugs and Pharmaceutical (NICDAP), at Central Drug Research Institute, Lucknow has been engaged to provide bibliographic support to enquiry made on Indian System of Medicine and Homoeopathy (ISM&H) drugs. Besides, the Central Institute of Medical and Aromatic Plants (CIMAP) is bringing out Current Research on Medical and Aromatic Plants (CROMAP), in computerized databases.

4.5 : Website of Department of Ayurveda, Yoga and Naturopathy, Unani, Siddha and Homoeopathy (AYUSH)

The beautiful website has already been created by the Department of Ayurveda, Yoga and Naturopathy, Unani, Siddha and Homoeopathy (AYUSH)[7]. This acts as the gateway for information on Indian Systems of Medicine and Homoeopathy brought for the public use.

5. Use of Internet for Indian System of Medicine and Homoeopathy (ISM&H)

Library can use INTERNET for providing information to the public who are interested for the Indian System of Medicine and Homoeopathy (ISM&H) in the rural areas and other parts of country in the following way :

(*a*) On-line searching of the List of Medical Institutions and doctors practicing the Indian System of Medicine and Homoeopathy (ISM&H).

(*b*) On-line booking of appointment to the doctor for patient's physical check-up.

(*c*) On-line appointment to the Hospital/Dispensary for treatment.

(*d*) On-line health information and advice to patients.

(*e*) On-line information for vacant bed in hospitals for admission of patient.

(*f*) Doctor patient interaction through e-mail/fax.

(*g*) On-line global information repository about available donors of blood and other organs.

With the help of Internet people can seek appointment for their treatment in the preferred ISM Hospital or mention his problem regarding disease and get appointments either their choice or as per suggestions of the Central System Management. For seeking appoint for treatment or bed patients may register himself/herself through the Internet as per Table 3. The Central System Management of ISM & H can respond or confirm the appointment as per Table 4.

The exchanging information between Patient and Hospitals/Doctors using Internet, as shown in Table 3 and Table 4, have some system to follow *i.e.* e-mail/fax/telephone information; name and address of the patient; case history; preferred system; medical college and its address and date of appointment, etc. The detail interaction method of exchanging information between patient and ISM Hospitals and confirmation of appointment for treatment are to be found in ISM & H Model 1.

6. The Model

The present Indian System of Medicine facilities has extended to the urban and rural people as Government principle. This opportunity will reach the people as quick as possible. For this purpose the advent of Information Technology should be adopted at the best. The procedure for confirming appointment to the patient seeking treatment for Indian System of Medicine may be served regularly with the help of IT. The schematic view of this service Indian System of Medicine (ISM&H) may be as under :

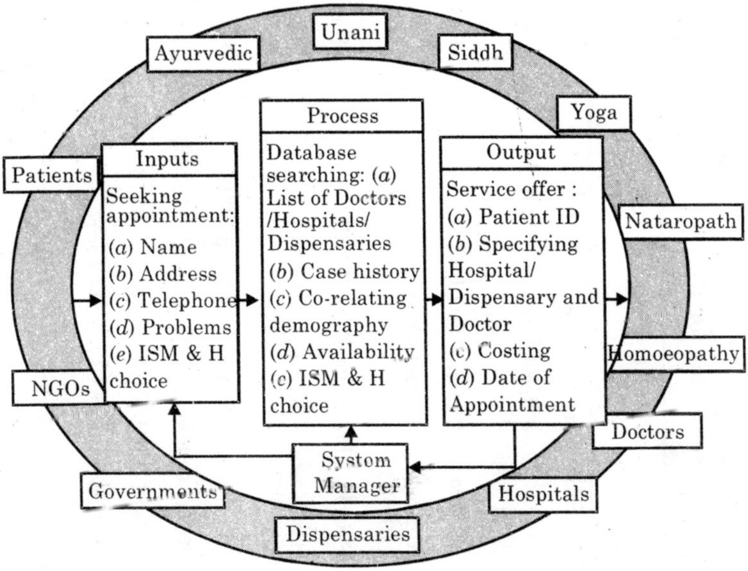

Model 1: Schematic view Management of Indian System of Medicine (ISM&H), Possible Appointment Services for the Patient within its environment.

The model shows the ISM&H environment, which is to be found here in blackish area where Ayurvedic, Unani, Siddha, Yoga, Naturopathy, and Homoeopathy System exists along with its doctors, hospitals, dispensaries, Government and Non-Government approaches for the treatment of patients. The model also shows the patients – ISM & H system interaction through imputs and outputs seeking oppointment for treatment and confirmation of appointment with other details.

Conclusion

The Indian Systems of Medicine have relied on medicinal plants available in the neighborhood areas. Knowledge about use of such medicinal plants and other easily available medicinal products (like condiments, herbs, etc.) passed on

Table 3 : Patient Seeking for Treatment for ISM & H

E-mail/Fax	*Name of the Patient*	*Address*	*Option for ISM&H System*
sknandi3@yahoo.co.in	Swapan Kr. Nandi	Santiniketan – 731235 West Bengal	Ayurveda
ksmalia@hotmail.com	Kali Sankar Malia	34, NK Bose Road Kolkata 700 012 West Bengal	Unani
aojha@rediffmail.com	Arun Ojha	AS Road, Aligarh – 202 002	Siddha
nisant@yahoo.co.in	Nisant Arora	A Block, Defence Colony, New Delhi–110 024	Yoga
bkpathi@yahoo.co.in	Bijay Kanta Pathi	Marchi Kote Lane Puri 752 001	Homoeopathy
rmenan@hotmail.com	Rajanish Menon	Irla Naka, Vile Parle Mumbay–400 056	Naturopathy
rksing@rediffmail.com	RK Sing	368, Koti Attanas Meerut 250 002	Ayurveda
Bjha12@yahoo.co.in	Baidyanath Pr. Jha	Millat Colony, Kanke Ranchi 834 006	Ayurveda
bdeka@rediffmail.com	Bijen Deka	Masjid Road Karimganja – 788710	Unani
sumana@yahoo.co.in	Sumana Mukherji	16/1, Boxi Gali Chandannagore-712 104	Homoeopathy

Table 4 : Hospital/Doctors Confirmation for Treatment

Patients E-Mail/Fax	*Hospital/Doctor*	*Address*	*Date Appinntment*
sknandi3@yahoo.co.in	Rashtriya Ayurveda Vidyapeeth	Dhanwantari Bhawana, Road No.66, West Punjabi Bagh, New Delhi - 700 026.	23/08/2004
ksmalia@hotmail.com	The Calcutta Unani Medical College & Hospital	8/1 Abdul Halim Lane, Kolkata-700016	22/08/2004
aojha@rediffmail.com	Government Unani Medical College	Himmatganj Allahabad–211 016	01/09/2004
nisant@yahoo.co.in	Bapu Nature Care Hospital and Yogashram	Patparganj, Delhi – 110 092	14/09/2004
bkpathi@yahoo.co.in	Biju Patanayak Homoeopathic Medical College & Hospital	Near City Hospital Road, Berhampur Ganjam – 769 010	09/09/2004
rmenan@hotmail.com	Bapu Nature Care Hospital and Yogashram	Patparganj, Delhi – 110 092	31/08/2004
rksing@rediffmail.com	Govt. Gurukul Kangri Ayurvedic College and Hospital	Hardwar – 249 404	12/09/2004
Bjha12@yahoo.co.in	Government Ayurvedic College	Kadam Kuaan, Patna – 800 003	1708/2004
bdeka@rediffmail.com	The Calcutta Unani Medical College and Hospital	8/1 Abdul Halim Lane, Kolkata-700016	02/08/2004
sumana@yahoo co.in	Burdwan Homoeopathic Hospital	Nutanganj, Burdwan - 713 101	09/09/2004

from generation to generation through the family elders. Because of pressure of population (1,02,70,15,247 in Census 2001), the cultivation of food grains and commercial crops, have progressively and practically eliminated locally growing medicinal plants. Again, because of the vast changes in the social system, the family traditions have also become weak. Another problem is that mentioning practices and cures, a deficiency of the ISM is that objective data through clinical trials and laboratory work has not been generated to prove the extent of efficacy of individual prescriptions/cures. The efficacy of ISM is to be established, if the cures mentioned in the texts are systematically taken up and subjected to laboratory investigation and clinical trials and then it will be highly beneficial to the society. Thus, the most effective cures out of the many recommended for a particular condition will be identified, which then can be propagated for extensive use for the benefit of patients.

So, Indian Systems of Medicine have a great role in Indian health care measures particularly in rural areas because 72.2% people are living in rural areas as reported in 2001 Census. In the rural areas medical services are to be provided for the people, through a network of integrated with the Allopathic System vis-à-vis Indian System of Medicine. If this practice of expansion can be adopted in real sense for the rural areas – the infrastructure for public health and medical care will be developed or boosted immediately, then "health for all" it is to be ensured, at least within 2020.

References

1. Chevallier, Andrew : Encyclopedia of Medicinal Plants. London: Dorling Kindersley, 2001.
2. India. Ministry of Health and Family Welfare. Department of ISM and Homoeopathy : Indian systems of medicine and homoeopathy in India 2001. New Delhi, 2002.
3. India. Ministry of Broadcasting : India 2003: a reference annual. New Delhi, 2003.
4. *Ibid.*, p. 241.
5. India. Ministry of Health and Family Welfare. *op. cit.*
6. http://www.indiamedicine.nic.in/showfile.asp?bid=316
7. http://india.gov.in/sectors/health-family/ayush/php

Index

Administrative responsibilities, 30, 31
Allopathic System, 121
American librarians, 9
Productivity Center, 77
Analysis, identification of library; identification of staff category; identification of job involvement, 23
Argyris, C., 13
Aronson, J., 84, 102
Assistance service, 40
Authority, responsibility to, 30
AYUSH, 129

B.L.I.S., 28
Berne Convention, 88, 89
Berrien, F.K., 8
Bigus, J.P., 102
Blum, M.L., 8
Bretthauer, David, 51
British Copyright Act of 1709, 87
Brown, J.M., 8
Brussels Convention of 1886, 92
Burdwan University Library, 23, 24

CAI (Computer assisted instruction), 65
Canadian librarians, 9
Carr-Saunders, A.M., 27
CD-ROMs, 41, 57, 64, 117
Central and State Governments, 34, 35
Changes in E-resources publishing, 107-110
Charaka, 122
Chemical Abstracts, 41
Civil Survival and Safe Motherhood (CSSM), 123
Code of Ethics, 29
Coleagues and other institution librarians, responsibility, 30
Conceptualizing profession, 26
Confucius, 55
Consortiums available in India, 59
for Indian Libraries, 63
Constrains, 43
Consumer Behaviour Approach, 118
Copyright and Library Association, 93
defined, 87
historical background, 87
library and library services, 87-95
Crown, 87
CSIR (Council of Scientific and Industrial Research), 128

Data compression, 101, 102
Data mining, 102
Davanport, T.H., 76
Deka, Dipen, 47
DeLong, David, 77
Development environment in library, need for, 36
Digital Image Acquisition Process, 99, 100
Digital Library programme, drives for the success, 42, 43
Digital Library, 37, 38, 39, 94
Doctrine of fair use, 93
Duhon, B., 76

Dunn, J.D., 10

E-books and E-reference books resources for Indian Libraries, 59, 62
E-databases (bibliographical) for Indian Libraries, 59, 62
Education (develop), responsibility, 32
E-Journal Websites, 58
  changed pricing systems, 111-116
E-library environment, 34-44
E-publications as helpful resources for researchers of Indian Libraries, 55-64
E-publishers and Indian Libraries, 56-59
E-resources available for Indian University Libraries, 109, 110
  for Indian libraries, 61
  types, 107-109
ERT, 97, 98
  files and recommended formats, 100
  process, 98-102
Executive Compensation Service of the American Management Association, 17
Expectations, 2, 3
Expected library services in changing environment, 39, 40

Fayol, H., 19
FOC, 69
French Republican Constitution, 88

Gateway Portals, 58
George P D'elia Study, 11
Grayson, C.J., 84
Greenwood, E., 27
Group studies in libraries, 19
  importance, 19, 20
Gulick, L.H., 19

Hardware, 98
Herzberg's theory, 9
Hussain, Rashid, 66
Hygiene factors, 10

ICT in Library and Information Science, 66
Indian Copyright Act (1999), 89, 93, 94
  law, 89
Indian Health Programme, 123
Indian Library Organisations, 25
Indian Patent Database, 57
Indian System of Medicine and Homoeopathy, 124
  origin, 121, 122
Indigenous medicine, traditional knowledge on, 122
Information and Communication Technology (ICT), 36, 37, 65-73
Information needs of people, 35, 36
Information System, 35
Information Technology (IT), 55, 56
  and KM, 78-80
INSDOC, 54
Instruction Service, 41
International library loan, 92
Internet, 65
ISM knowledge, preservation of, 127-129
ISM & H doctors, 125, 126, 129, 130, 131, 132, 134, 136

Job, definition, 8
Job description Index, 10
Job enlargement, 13
Job enrichment, 13
Job means, 7, 8
Job rotation, 13
Job satisfactions, 7-14
  methods of increasing, 8, 12
  studies on, 9

Jones and Jordan on the issue, 11
Jones, N., 7
Jordan, E.P., 7

Keystone Principles, 45
Knod, E., 13
Knowledge Management (KM), definition, 76
  for University Libraries, 82-84
  in libraries, need, 81, 82
  in Library and Information Centre, 75-85
  managers, task of, 78
  preservation indigenous system of medicine, 121-137
  versus Library and Information Management, 80, 81

LAN, 69, 79
Librarian and Publishers, 93
Librarian's role in changed environment, 103, 116-119
  and E-publications, 59, 60
  and ICT, 66
  and other organizations, problems solving action, 92-94
Librarianship a profession, is, 28, 29
Libraries, applications, 4
Library and concept of organizational module, 16, 17
Library and Copyrighted materials, 90
Library and Electronic Recording Technology (ERT), 99-105
Library and information services, changing dimensions of, 34-44
Library and its employee, 1, 2
Library manager, 1
Library working group, 16-25
Library associations, 32
Library environment, changing, 38, 39
Library in various way, 91
Library Law, 29
Library management, 18, 19
  current trends, 1-5
Library manager, role, 3
Library Organisation, objectives, 20
  study, 21, 22
Library profession (develop), responsibility to, 31
Library profession and its code of ethics, 26-33
Library professionals in ICT, 67, 68
  job satisfaction, 7-14
Library services, problems, 91, 92
Library, changing situations, 37
Library, non-profit service organization, 91
Licensing Act, 87
Linux operating system, 48
LISE, 66
Luthans, F., 13

M.L.I.S., 28
Maclver, R., 28
Management, middle, 18
  supervisory, 18
  top, 18
Managing University Library in changing environment, 106-119
McCormick, Ernest J., 8
McCune, C., 78
McGregor's theory (X & Y), 3, 4
McKay Sharon Cline, 118
Medicinal Plants Board, 127
Middle Ages, 16
Morgan, E.L., 51
Motivational factors, 9, 10

NASSADOC, 54
National Library, 54
Naylor, J.C., 8
New library environments, 55

O'Dell, C., 84
Occupational professionalism, 26
OCR (Optical Character Recognition), 102, 103

Open software, 45
Open Source Softwares, 45-52
  and Visva-Bharati Library, 50
  certification, 46, 47
  definition, 46
  features, 47
  Indian Scenario, 49
  library usage, 48, 49, 50
  users rights, 48
Organisational pyramid of an organization, 19, 23
Organisational staff position, 17
OSI (Open Source Initiative), 46, 47

Plate and Stone Study, 9
Plate, K.H., 14
Pricing pattern, changes, 110, 111
Problems, 12
Profession, definition, 26, 27, 28
Property and finance responsibility to, 31
Public Library, 35

R&D (research and development), 77
Ranganathan, S.R., 28, 77, 80
Readers' Guide, 41
Readers'/users' part, changing situations, 38
Reciprocal relationship, 2
Redesign of library system, need for, 54, 55
Referral services, 42
Research, means, 55
Right to Information Act (2005), 34, 35
Ruggles, R., 76
Russell, D.L., 8

Sayood, K., 101
Samhita, Susruta, 122
Schematic presentation of working groups of library organization, 24
Seemann, Patrica, 77
Selection of libraries, 20
Self-enrichment, 31
Self-service, 40
Senior Librarians and TME, 71
Sheffield Manpower Project Study, 9
Simon, B.V., 17
Software, 98
Stone, E.W., 14

Tarban, E., 102
Tiffin, Joseph, 8
TME model, 71
Traditional library system and research, 54
  to Digital Library (change from), 37, 38
Training methods, 68-72
TRIPS agreement, 89
Turban, E., 84, 102

UNESCO, 92
United States Constitution in 1787, 88
University Libraries, environmental changes, 99
University People, basic information needs, 36
Urwick, L., 19
Users, responsibility to, 30

Vass, L., 84
Vaughn and Dunn Study, 10
Vaughn, W.J., 10
Visva-Bharati University Library, 23, 24, 69

Wabha Study, 10
WAN, 79
WHO, 123
Wright, Peter, 65

Yellow Pages, 79